D1460413

The Observer's Pocket Series

AUTOMOBILES

Observer's Books

NATURAL HISTORY
Birds • Birds' Eggs • Wild Animals • Zoo Animals
Farm Animals • Freshwater Fishes • Sea Fishes
Tropical Fishes • Butterflies • Larger Moths
Caterpillars • Insects • Pond Life • Sea and Seashore
Seashells • Pets • Dogs • Horses and Ponies • Cats
Trees • Wild Flowers • Grasses • Mushrooms • Lichens
Cacti • Garden Flowers • Flowering Shrubs • Vegetables
House Plants • Geology • Rocks and Minerals • Fossils
Weather • Astronomy

SPORT
Soccer • Cricket • Golf • Tennis • Coarse Fishing
Fly Fishing • Show Jumping • Motor Sport

TRANSPORT
Automobiles • Aircraft • Commercial Vehicles
Motorcycles • Steam Locomotives • Ships • Small Craft
Manned Spaceflight • Unmanned Spaceflight

ARCHITECTURE
Architecture • Churches • Cathedrals • Castles

COLLECTING
Awards and Medals • Coins • Firearms • Furniture
Postage Stamps • Glass • Pottery and Porcelain

ARTS AND CRAFTS
Music • Painting • Modern Art • Sewing • Jazz
Big Bands

HISTORY AND GENERAL INTEREST
Ancient Britain • Flags • Heraldry • European Costume

TRAVEL
London • Tourist Atlas GB • Lake District • Cotswolds

The Observer's Book of

AUTOMOBILES

Compiled by the
OLYSLAGER ORGANISATION

FREDERICK WARNE
LONDON

First Edition 1955
Twenty-second Edition 1979

NOTE

The specifications contained in this book were collated on the basis of material available to the compilers up to the end of October 1978. All information is subject to change and/or cancellation during the course of the model year. Although every effort has been made to ensure correctness in compiling this book, responsibility for inaccuracies and omissions cannot be accepted by the compilers and publishers.

LIBRARY OF CONGRESS CATALOG
CARD NO. 62–9807

ISBN 0 7232 1595 2

Printed and bound in Great Britain at
William Clowes & Sons Limited
Beccles and London

KEY TO DATA

1. Engine. Engine location, number and layout of cylinders are given. Valve actuation is either by means of a camshaft and push rods (ohv) or by a direct-acting overhead camshaft (ohc). Rotary and two-stroke engines do not have valves.

Bore (cylinder diameter) and stroke (piston travel) are quoted in millimetres. To convert to inches multiply by 0.03937.

Output is quoted in Kilowatts which is now the accepted measurement in the EEC.

Torque (twisting effort by the engine) is quoted in Newton Metres for the same reason.

A table is shown below for those readers wishing to convert to more familiar terminology.

NEWTON METRES (Nm) =

1 Nm = 0,7233 ft. lbs.

1 ft. lb. = 1,3825 Nm   1 Mkg = 10 Nm

	0	1	2	3	4
—	—	,7233	1,4466	2,1699	2,8932
10	7,2330	7,9563	8,6796	9,4029	10,1262
20	14,4660	15,1893	15,9126	16,6359	17,3592
30	21,6990	22,4223	23,1456	23,8689	24,5922
40	28,9320	29,6553	30,3786	31,3019	31,8252
50	36,1650	26,8883	37,6116	38,3349	39,0582
60	43,3980	44,1213	44,8446	45,5679	46,2912
70	50,6310	51,3543	52,0776	52,8009	53,5242
80	57,8640	58,5873	59,3106	60,0339	60,7572
90	65,0970	65,8203	66,5436	67,2669	67,9902

FOOT POUNDS

5	6	7	8	9	
3,615	4,3398	5,0631	5,7864	6,5097	–
10,8495	11,5728	12,2961	13,0194	13,7427	10
18,0825	18,8058	19,5921	20,2524	20,9759	20
25,3155	26,0388	26,7621	27,4854	28,2087	30
32,5485	33,2718	33,9951	34,7184	35,4417	40
39,7815	40,5038	41,2281	41,9514	42,6747	50
47,0145	47,7378	48,4611	49,1844	49,9077	60
54,2475	54,9708	55,6941	56,4174	57,1407	70
61,4805	62,2038	62,9271	63,6504	64,3737	80
68,7135	69,4368	70,1601	70,8834	71,6067	90

KILOWATTS (Kw) =

1 Kw = 1.3369 bhp (DIN)
1 bhp (DIN) = 0.748 Kw

	0	1	2	3	4
–	–	1,3369	2,6738	4,0107	5,3476
10	13,3690	14,7059	16,0428	17,3797	18,7166
20	26,7380	28,0749	29,4118	20,7487	32,0856
30	40,1070	41,4438	42,7808	44,1177	45,4546
40	53,4760	54,8129	56,1498	57,4867	58,8236
50	66,8450	68,1819	69,5188	70,8557	72,1926
60	80,2140	81,5509	82,8878	84,2247	85,5616
70	93,5830	94,9199	96,2568	97,5937	98,9306
80	106,9520	108,2889	109,6258	110,9627	112,2996
90	120,3210	121,6579	122,9948	124,3317	125,6686

BHP (DIN)

5	6	7	8	9	
6,6845	8,0214	9,3583	10,6952	12,0321	—
20,0535	21,3904	22,7273	24,0642	25,4011	10
33,4225	34,7594	36,0963	37,4332	38,7701	20
46,7915	48,1284	49,4653	50,8022	52,1391	30
60,1605	61,4974	62,8343	64,1712	65,5081	40
73,5295	74,8664	76,2033	77,5402	78,8771	50
86,8985	88,2354	89,5723	90,9092	92,2461	60
100,2675	101,6044	102,9413	104,2782	105,6151	70
113,6365	114,9734	116,3103	117,6472	118,9841	80
127,0055	128,3424	129,6793	131,0162	132,3531	90

2.   Engine Size. Engine size is quoted in cubic centimetres for the standard engine of the model shown.

3.   Carburettor. 'Single' means one carburettor even though it may have one, two or even four barrels.
Where fuel-injection is used this receives a special mention.

4.   Transmission. This can be through the front wheels, rear wheels or on   some recent models all four wheels.
The number of speeds in a manual gearbox are quoted and where applicable an automatic transmission.

5.   Brakes. The growing use of disc brakes and servo-assistance will be apparant to readers of earlier Observer books. Disc brakes on front and rear are featured on many high performance and top-line models.

They have a much greater resistance to fade than drum brakes and do not require greater pedal pressure if no servo-assistance is fitted.

6.   Steering. Use of rack and pinion or re-circulating ball is now almost universal — the former preferred by European and the latter by North American manufacturers.
Power assistance is offered on the top-line and heavier models.

7.   Suspension. Front wheels are independently sprung with only very few exceptions. Springs used are usually of the coil or torsion bar type — the former either with wishbones of unequal length or combined with shock absorbers forming a "suspension strut".
Some cars have transversal leaf springs, other notable exceptions being some British Leyland models which employ the "Hydrolastic" rubber-and-fluid system interconnecting the front and rear suspension at each side, and the larger Citroens which feature a sophisticated self-levelling hydro-pneumatic system.

Most American and Japense manufacturers rely on the conventional "live" rear axle layout whereby the car is suspended by means of either semi-elliptical single or multi-leaf springs or coil springs. In Europe the tendency is towards an independent rear suspension system in various configurations. Some top-of-the-range models use self-levelling devices.

8. Tyres. Sizes quoted are for the standard fitment for the model shown; model variations may have different tyres.
Radial-ply tyres are now predominant although cross-ply and belted-bias still to be found — especially in North America.

Tyre coding presents a bewildering variety. As a rule, tyre width is quoted 5.20, 6.00 etc in inches or 155, 185 etc in mm. Wheel rims similarly are quoted 13, 15 etc in inches or 330, 380 etc in mm.

9. Dimensions. Overall dimensions are quoted in mm.

10. Wheelbase. is the distance between front and rear wheel centres.

11. Weight. The unladen weight is normally the manufacturers kerb weight and is quoted in kilogrammes (Kg).
The variety of ways by which the kerb weight is calculated means that figures must be taken as a rough guide to the vehicle's weight without driver, passengers or luggage.

12. Capacities. Metric measures are given followed by Imperial measures in brackets. To convert from Imperial to US gallons or pints multiply by 1.2. Some engines are air-cooled and of course no cooling system capacities are given in such cases Fuel tank capacities include any reserve tank(s) where fitted.

ALFASUD N $1186\ cm^3$

Engine— water-cooled, 4-cylinder, flat engine, front mounted, bore x stroke 80 x 59, displacement 1186 cm^3 2 ohc, compression ratio 8.8:1, max. power 46 kW (63 bhp) at 6000/min, max. torque 88 Nm (65 lbf.ft) at 3200/min, 1 Solex carburettor.
Transmission—front wheels, 4-speed gearbox.
Steering—rack and pinion.
Suspension—front/rear McPherson struts, dead axle with Panhard rod.
Springs—coil springs and telescopic shock absorbers front and rear.
Brakes—front/rear discs, servo-assisted.
Dimensions and weights—length 3890mm, width 1590mm, height 1370mm, wheelbase 2455mm, kerb weight 860 kg.
Tyres—145 SR 13.
Capacities--engine sump 4 litres (7 Imp. pints), cooling system 7.3 litres (13 Imp. pints), fuel tank 50 litres (11 Imp. gal).
  Notes—Top speed 150 km/h (93 mph)

ALFA ROMEO GIULIETTA 1.6   1570 cm^3

Engine—water-cooled, 4-cylinder, in-line, front mounted,
bore x stroke 78 x 82, displacement 1570 cm^3, 2 x ohc,
compression ratio 9:1, max. power 80 kW (109 bhp) at
5600/min, max. torque 142 Nm (105 lbf.ft) at 4300/min,
Transmission—rear wheels; 5-speed gearbox.
Steering—rack and pinion.
Suspension—front/rear independent trailing arms with
torsion bars and anti-roll bar. De Dion axle.
Springs—front: torsion bars, rear: coil springs and
telescopic shock absorbers front and rear.
Brakes—front/rear discs,
Dimensions and weights—length 4210mm, width 1650mm
height 1400mm, wheelbase 2510mm, kerb weight 1070kg.
Tyres—165 SR 13.
Capacities—engine sump 6.5 litres (11.50 Imp. pints),
cooling system 8 litres (14 Imp. pints), fuel tank 50 litres
(11 Imp. gal).
   Notes—Top speed 175 km/h (109 mph).

ALFA ROMEO ALFETTA 2000   1962 cm^3

Engine—water-cooled, 4-cylinder, in-line, front mounted, bore x stroke 84 x 88.5, displacement 1962 cm^3, 2 ohc, compression ratio 9:1, max. power 90 kW (122 bhp) at 5300/min, max. torque 176 Nm (130 lbf.ft) at 4000/min 2 Solex or Dell'Orto carburettors.
Transmission—rear wheels, 5-speed gearbox.
Steering—rack and pinion.
Suspension—front/rear independent wishbones with anti-roll bar. De Dion axle.
Springs—front torsion bars, rear coil springs and telescopic shock absorbers front and rear.
Brakes—front/rear discs, servo-assisted.
Dimensions and weights—length 4385, USA 4380mm, width 1640mm, height 1430mm, wheelbase 2510mm, kerb weight 1140, USA 1220 kg.
Tyres—165 SR 14 or 185/70 HR 14.
Capacities—engine sump 5.5 litres (9.75 Imp. pints), cooling system 9.7 litres (17 Imp. pints), fuel tank 49 litres (10.75 Imp. gal).
  Notes—USA version with SPICA - fuel injection: 82.5 kW at 5500/min.
  Notes—Top speed 190 km/h (118 mph)

ALFA ROMEO ALFASUD SPRINT 1.5   1490 cm^3

Engine—water-cooled, 4-cylinder, flat engine, front mounted
bore x stroke 84 x 67.2, displacement 1490 cm^3, 2 ohc,
compression ratio 9:1, max. power 63 kW (86 bhp) at
5800/min, max. torque 121 Nm (89 lbf.ft) at 3500/min,
1 Weber carburettor.
Transmission—front wheels, 5-speed gearbox.
Steering—rack and pinion.
Suspension—front/rear McPherson struts, dead axle with
Panhard rod.
Springs—coil springs and telescopic shock absorbers front
and rear.
Brakes—front/rear discs, servo-assisted.
Dimensions and weights—length 4020mm, width 1610mm
height 1305mm, wheelbase 2455mm, kerb weight 890 kg.
Tyres—165/70 SR 13.
Capacities—engine sump 4 litres (7 Imp. pints), cooling
system 7.3 litres (13 Imp. pints), fuel tank 50 litres
(11 Imp. gal).
  Notes—Top speed 170 km/h (105 mph)

ALFA ROMEO 2000 SPIDER VELOCE 1962 cm^3

Engine—water-cooled, 4-cylinder, in-line, front mounted, bore x stroke 84 x 88.5, displacement 1962 cm^3, 2 ohc, compression ratio 9:1, max. power 94 kW (128 bhp) at 5300/min, max. torque 178 Nm (131 lbf.ft) at 3500/min, 2 Solex or Dell'Orto carburettors.
Transmission—rear wheels, 5-speed gearbox.
Steering—worm and roller.
Suspension—front/rear independent wishbones with anti-roll bar. Dead axle,
Springs—coil springs and telescopic shock absorbers front and rear.
Brakes—front/rear discs, servo-assisted.
Dimensions and weights—length 4120, USA 4220mm, width 1630mm, height 1290mm, wheelbase 2250mm, kerb weight 1040, USA 1100 kg.
Tyres—165 HR 14.
Capacities—engine sump 7.2 litres (12.50 Imp. pints), cooling system 9.7 litres (17 Imp. pints), fuel tank 51 litres (11.25 Imp gal).
   Notes—Top speed 195 km/h (121 mph)

ALPINE RENAULT A 310 V6   2664 cm^3

Engine—water-cooled, V6, rear-mounted, bore x stroke
88 x 73, displacement 2664 cm^3, 2 ohc, compression ratio
10.1:1, max. power 111 kW (151 bhp) at 6000/min, max.
torque 204 Nm (151 lbf.ft) at 3500/min, Solex single and
double carburettor.
Transmission—rear wheels, 4-speed gearbox.
Steering—rack and pinion.
Suspension—independent wishbones with anti-roll bar,
independent trailing arms.
Springs—coil springs and telescopic shock absorbers front
and rear.
Brakes—front/rear discs, servo-assisted.
Dimensions and weights—length 4180mm, width 1640mm
height 1150mm, wheelbase 2270mm, kerb weight 1020 kg.
Tyres—front/rear 185/70 VR13/ 205/70 VR 13.
Capacities—engine sump 6 litres (10.50 Imp. pints),
cooling system 12 litres (21 Imp. pints), fuel tank 63
litres (14 Imp. gal).
   Notes—Top speed 220 km/h (136 mph)

AMC CONCORD 3.8   3802 cm^3

Engine—water-cooled, 6-cylinder, in-line, front mounted,
bore x stroke 95.25 x 88.9, displacement 3802 cm^3, 1 ohv
compression ratio 8:1, max. power 67 kW (91 bhp) at
3400/min, max. torque 228 Nm (168 lbf.ft) at 1600/min.
1 Carter single carburettor.
Transmission—rear wheels. 3-speed gearbox.
Steering—recirculating ball.
Suspension—front/rear independent wishbones with anti-
roll bar dead axle.
Springs—front: coil springs, rear: leaf springs, telescopic
shock absorbers front and rear.
Brakes—front/rear, disc/drums.
Dimensions and weights—length 4660mm, width 1810mm
height 1310mm, wheelbase 2475mm, kerb weight 1405kg
Tyres—front/rear 185 SR/HR 14 ZX/175 SR/HR 14 ZX.
Capacities—engine sump 4.7 litres (8.25 Imp. pints),
cooling system 10.4 litres (18.25 Imp. pints), fuel tank
83 litres (18.25 Imp. gal).
   Notes—Top speed 150 km/h (93 mph)

ASTON MARTIN LAGONDA   5340 cm^3

Engine—water-cooled, V8, front mounted, bore x stroke 100 x 85, displacement 5340 cm^3, 2x2 ohc, compression ratio 9:1, max. power 276 kW (375 bhp) at 5500/min, torque 539 Nm (398 lbf.ft) at 4500/max. min, 4 Weber double carburettors.
Transmission—rear wheels; Chrysler automatic transmission.
Steering—rack and pinion, servo-assisted.
Suspension—front/rear independent wishbones with anti-roll bar/ De Dion axle.
Springs—coil springs and telescopic shock absorbers front and rear (rear level control).
Brakes—front/rear discs, servo-assisted.
Dimensions and weights—length 5285mm, width 1815mm, height 1300mm, wheelbase 2915mm, kerb weight 1725kg.
Tyres—GR 70 VR 15.
Capacities—engine sump 11.4 litres (20 Imp. pints), cooling system 17 litres (30 Imp. pints), fuel tank 128 litres (28 Imp. gal).
   Notes—V8 will be delivered as a Convertible from 1979 in the United Kingdom.
   Notes—Top speed 225 km/h (140 mph)

AUDI 80L   1272 cm³

Engine—water-cooled, 4-cylinder, in-line, front mounted, bore x stroke 75 × 72, displacement 1272 cm³, ohc, compression ratio 8.2:1, max. power 44 kW (60 bhp) at 5800/min, max. torque 95 Nm (70 lbf.ft) at 3800/min, 1 Solex single carburettor.
Transmission—front wheels; 4-speed gearbox.
Steering—rack and pinion.
Suspension—front/rear McPherson struts/semi-independent
Springs—coil springs and telescopic shock absorbers front and rear.
Brakes—front/rear discs/drums, servo-assisted.
Dimensions and weights—length 4383m, width 1682mm, height 1365mm, wheelbase 2541mm, kerb weight 910kg.
Tyres—155 SR 13.
Capacities—engine sump 3.5 litres (6 Imp. pints), cooling system 6 litres (10.50 Imp. pints), fuel tank 68 litres (15 Imp. gal).
  Notes—Top speed 165 km/h (102 mph).

AUDI 80 GLS
1588 cm^3

Engine—water-cooled, 4-cylinder, in-line, front mounted, bore x stroke 79.5 x 80, displacement 1588 cm^3, ohc, compression ratio 8.2:1, max. power 63 kW (86 bhp) at 5600/min, max. torque 127 Nm (94 lbf.ft) at 3200/min, 1 Solex single carburettor.
Transmission—front wheels; 4-speed gearbox.
Steering—rack and pinion.
Suspension—front/rear McPherson struts with anti-roll bar semi-independent.
Springs—coil springs and telescopic shock absorbers front and rear.
Brakes—front/rear discs/drums, servo-assisted.
Dimensions and weights—length 4383mm, width 1682mm height 1365mm, wheelbase 2541mm, kerb weight 950 kg.
Tyres—175/70 SR 13.
Capacities—engine sump 3 litres (5.25 Imp. pints), cooling system 6.2 litres (11 Imp. pints), fuel tank 68 litres (15 Imp. gal).
　Notes—Top speed 165 km/h (102 mph).

AUDI 100L 5S

2144 cm^3

Engine—water-cooled, 5-cylinder, in-line, front mounted, bore x stroke 79.5 x 86.4, displacement 2144 cm^3, 1 ohc, compression ratio 8.3:1, max. power 85 kW (116 bhp) at 5500/min, max. torque 166 Nm (123 lbf.ft) at 4000/min. 1 Zenith carburettor.

Transmission—front wheels. 4-speed gearbox/Automatic transmission.

Steering—rack and pinion;

Suspension—front/rear McPherson struts with anti-roll bar, semi-independent with Panhard rod.

Springs—coil springs and telescopic shock absorbers front and rear.

Brakes—front/rear discs/drums, servo-assisted.

Dimensions and weights—length 4860mm, width 1768mm, height 1390mm, wheelbase 2677mm, kerb weight 1185kg.

Tyres—165 SR 14.

Capacities—engine sump 4.5 litres (8 Imp. pints), ccoling system 8.1 litres (14.25 Imp. pints) fuel tank 60 litres (13.25 Imp. gal).

   Notes—Top speed 177 km/h (110 mph)

AUDI 100 AVANT GL 5E   2144 cm^3

Engine—water-cooled, 5-cylinder, in-line, front mounted, bore x stroke 79.5 x 86.4, displacement 2144 cm^3, 1 ohc, compression ratio 9.3:1, max. power 100 kW (136 bhp) at 5700/min, max. torque 182 Nm (134 lbf.ft) at 4200/min; Bosch K-Jetronic fuel injection.
Transmission—front wheels, 4-speed gearbox.
Steering—rack and pinion, servo-assisted.
Suspension—front/rear McPherson struts with anti-roll bar, semi-independent with Panhard rod.
Springs—coil springs and telescopic shock absorbers front and rear.
Brakes—front/rear discs/drums, servo-assisted.
Dimensions and weights—length 4607mm, width 1768mm, height 1390mm, wheelbase 2677mm, kerb weight 1170kg.
Tyres—185/70 HR 14.
Capacities—engine sump 4.5 litres (8 Imp. pints), cooling system 8.1 litres (14.25 Imp. pints), fuel tank 60 litres (13.25 Imp. gal).
    Notes—Top speed 190 km/h (118 mph)

AUSTIN ALLEGRO 1500 SPECIAL   1485 cm^3

Engine—water-cooled, 4-cylinder, in line, front mounted,
bore x stroke 76.2 x 81.3, displacement 1485 cm^3, ohv,
compression ratio 9:1, max. power 50 kW (68 bhp) at
5500/min, max. torque 109 Nm (80 lbf.ft) at 2900/min,
1 SU carburettor.
Transmission—front wheels; 5-speed gearbox.
Steering—rack and pinion.
Suspension—front/rear independent wishbones,
independent trailing arms.
Springs—"Hydragas" system front and rear.
Brakes—front/rear discs/drums, servo-assisted.
Dimensions and weights—length 3850mm, width 1615mm
height 1390mm, wheelbase 2440mm, kerb weight 870 kg.
Tyres—145 SR13.
Capacities—engine sump 5.5 litres (9.75 Imp. pints),
cooling system 6.5 litres (11.50 Imp. pints), fuel tank
48 litres (10.50 Imp. gal).
  Notes—Top speed 148 km/h (92 mph)

AUSTIN MAXI 1750HL

1748 cm³

Engine—water-cooled, 4 cylinder, in-line, front mounted, bore x stroke 76.2 x 95.7, displacement 1748 cm³ ohv compression ratio 9.5:1, max. power 67 kW (91 bhp) at 5250/min, max. torque 141 Nm (104 lbf.ft) at 3400/min 2 SU carburettors.
Transmission—front wheels; 5-speed gearbox.
Steering—rack and pinion.
Suspension—front/rear independent wishbones, independent trailing arms.
Springs—"Hydragas" system and telescopic shock absorbers front and rear.
Brakes—front/rear discs/drums, servo-assisted.
Dimensions and weights—length 4020mm, width 1630mm height 1404mm, wheelbase 2640mm, kerb weight 1005kg.
Tyres—165 SR 13.
Capacities—engine sump 5.6 litres (9.75 Imp. pints), cooling system 5.2 litres (9.1 Imp. pints), fuel tank 41 litres (9 Imp. gal.)
  Notes—Top speed 157 km/h (97 mph)

AUTO-BIANCHI A112 ABARTH   1049 cm^3

Engine—water-cooled, 4-cylinder, in-line, front mounted, bore x stroke 67.2 x 74, displacement 1049 cm^3, 1 ohv, compression ratio 10.4:1, max. power 51 kW (69 bhp) at 6660/min, max. torque 85 Nm (63 lbf ft) at 4200/min, 1 Weber double carburettor.
Transmission—front wheels, .
Steering—rack and pinion.
Suspension—front/rear McPherson struts , anti-roll bar independent trailing arms.
Springs—front coil springs, rear transversal leaf springs, telescopic shock absorbers front and rear.
Brakes—front/rear discs/drums, servo-assisted.
Dimensions and weights—length 3203mm, width 1480 mm, height 1360mm, wheelbase 2038mm, kerb weight 672 kg.
Tyres—135 SR 13.
Capacities—engine sump 4.2 litres (7.50 Imp. pints), cooling system 5 litres (8.75 Imp. pints), fuel tank 30 litres (6.50 Imp. gal).
  Notes—Top speed 160 km/h (99 mph)

BENTLEY T2 SALOON $6750\ cm^3$

Engine—water-cooled, V8 front mounted, bore x stroke 104.1 x 99.1, displacement $6750\ cm^3$, ohv, compression ratio 8:1, max. power and max. torque not quoted by manufacturer, 2 SU carburettors.

Transmission—rear wheels; GM, automatic transmission .

Steering—rack and pinion, servo-assisted.

Suspension—front/rear independent wishbones with anti-roll bar, independent trailing arms.

Springs—coil springs and telescopic shock absorbers front and rear. Automatic levelling control front and rear.

Brakes—front/rear discs, servo-assisted.

Dimensions and weights—length 5170mm, width 1800mm, height 1520mm, wheelbase 3030mm, kerb weight 2160kg.

Tyres—235/70 HR 15.

Capacities—engine sump 8.3 litres (14.50 Imp. pints), cooling system 16.2 litres (28.50 Imp. pints), fuel tank 107 litres (23 Imp. gal).

   Notes—Top speed 195 km/h (121 mph)

BMW 316   1573 cm^3

Engine—water-cooled, 4-cylinder, in-line, front mounted, bore x stroke 84 x 71, displacement 1573 cm^3, 1 ohc compression ratio 8.3:1, max. power 66 kW (90 bhp) at 6000/min, max. torque 123 Nm (91 lbf.ft) at 4000/min 1 Solex carburettor.
Transmission—rear wheels; 4-speed gearbox.
Steering—rack and pinion.
Suspension—front/rear McPherson struts with anti-roll bar, independent trailing arms.
Springs—coil springs, auxiliary rubber springs and telescopic shock absorbers front and rear.
Brakes—front/rear discs/drums, servo-assisted.
Dimensions and weights—length 4355mm, width 1610mm, height 1380mm, wheelbase 2563mm, kerb weight 1020kg.
Tyres—165 SR 13.
Capacities—engine sump 4.25 litres (7.25 Imp. pints), cooling system 7.2 litres (12.50 Imp. pints), fuel tank 58 litres (12.75 Imp. gal).
  Notes—Also available is a Cabriolet version.
  Notes—Top speed 160 km/h (99 mph)

BMW 320 1990 cm^3

Engine—water-cooled, 6-cylinder, in-line, front mounted, bore x stroke 80 x 66, displacement 1990 cm^3, 1 ohc, compression ratio 9.2:1, max. power 90 kW (122 bhp) at 6000/min, max. torque 160 Nm (118 lbf.ft) at 4000/min 1 Solex double carburettor.

Transmission—rear wheels. 4-speed gearbox.

Steering—rack and pinion.

Suspension—front/rear McPherson struts with anti-roll bar, independent trailing arms.

Springs—coil springs, auxiliary rubber springs and telescopic shock absorbers front and rear.

Brakes—front/rear discs/drums, servo-assisted.

Dimensions and weights—length 4355mm, width 1610 mm, height 1380mm, wheelbase 2563mm, kerb weight 1115 kg.

Tyres—185/70 HR 13.

Capacities—engine sump 4.75 litres (8.25 Imp. pints), cooling system 12 litres (21 Imp. pints), fuel tank 58 litres (12.75 Imp. gal).

  Notes—Also available on request is a Cabriolet version. only for USA: 320i (82,5 kW, 170 km/h). The length is 4510mm. Can be delivered with 4- or 5-speed gearbox or automatic transmission (3-speed).

  Notes—Top speed 112 mph (181 km/h)

BMW 323 i   2315 cm^3

Engine—water-cooled, 6-cylinder, in-line, front mounted,
bore x stroke 80 x 76.5, displacement 2315 cm^3, 1 ohc,
compression ratio 9.5:1, max. power 105 kW (143 bhp)
at 6000/min, max. torque 190 Nm (140 lbf.ft) at 4500/
min, fuel-injection Bosch K-Jetronic.
Transmission—rear wheels; 4-speed gearbox.
Steering—rack and pinion.
Suspension—front/rear McPherson struts with anti-roll
bar, independent trailing arms.
Springs—coil springs, auxiliary rubber springs and
telescopic shock absorbers front and rear.
Brakes—front/rear discs/drums, servo-assisted.
Dimensions and weights—length 4355mm, width 1610mm
height 1380mm, wheelbase 2563mm, kerb weight 1135kg.
Tyres—185/70 HR 13.
Capacities—engine sump 4.75 litres (8.25 Imp pints),
cooling system 12 litres (21 Imp. pints), fuel tank
58 litres (12.50 Imp. gal).
   Notes—Also available is a Cabriolet version.
   Notes—Top speed 190 km/h (118 mph)

BMW 525

2494 cm^3

Engine—water-cooled, 6-cylinder, in-line, front mounted, bore x stroke 86 x 71.6, displacement 2494 cm^3, 1 ohc, compression ratio 9.0:1, max. power 110 kW (150 bhp) at 6000/min, max. torque 208 Nm (154 lbf.ft) at 4000/min, 1 Solex double carburettor.
Transmission—rear wheels. 4-speed gearbox.
Steering—worm and roller, servo-assisted.
Suspension—front/rear McPherson struts with anti-roll bar, independent trailing arms.
Springs—coil springs, auxiliary rubber springs and telescopic shock absorbers front and rear.
Brakes—front/rear discs, servo-assisted.
Dimensions and weights—length 4620mm, width 1690mm, height 1425mm, wheelbase 2636mm, kerb weight 1350kg.
Tyres—175 HR 14.
Capacities—engine sump 5.75 litres (10 Imp. pints), cooling system 12 litres (21 Imp. pints), fuel tank 70 litres (15.50 Imp. gal).
   Notes—Top speed 193 km/h (120 mph)

BMW 728   2788 cm^3

Engine—water-cooled, 6-cylinder, in-line, front mounted, bore x stroke 86 x 88, displacement 2788 cm^3, 1 ohc, compression ratio 9:1, max. power 125 kW (170 bhp) at 5800/min, max. torque 233 Nm (172 lbf.ft) at 4000/min 1 Solex double carburettor.
Transmission—rear wheels. 4-speed gearbox.
Steering—worm and roller, servo-assisted.
Suspension—front/rear McPherson struts with anti-roll bar, independent trailing arms.
Springs—coil springs, auxiliary rubber springs and telescopic shock absorbers front and rear.
Brakes—front/rear discs, servo-assisted.
Dimensions and weights—length 4860mm, width 1800mm height 1430mm, wheelbase 2795mm, kerb weight 1530kg.
Tyres—195/70 HR 14.
Capacities—engine sump 5.75 litres (10 Imp. pints), cooling system 12.4 litres (22 Imp. pints), fuel tank 85 litres (18.75 Imp. gal).
   Notes—Top speed 192 km/h (119 mph)

BMW 635 CSi

3453 cm^3

Engine—water-cooled, 6-cylinder, in-line, front mounted, bore x stroke 93 x 84, displacement 3453 cm^3, ohc, compression ratio 9.3:1, max. power 160 kW (218 bhp) at 5200/min, max. torque 310 Nm (229 lbf.ft) at 4000/min, fuel injection Bosch L-Jetronic.
Transmission—rear wheels; 5-speed gearbox.
Steering—recirculating ball, servo-assisted.
Suspension—front/rear McPherson struts with anti-roll bar, independent trailing arms.
Springs—coil, springs, auxiliary rubber springs and telescopic shock absorbers front and rear.
Brakes—front/rear discs, servo-assisted.
Dimensions and weights—length 4755mm, width 1725 mm, height 1365mm, wheelbase 2626mm, kerb weight 1500 kg.
Tyres—195/70 VR 14.
Capacities—fuel tank 70 litres (15.50 Imp. gal).
  Notes—Top speed 222 km/h. (138 mph)

BUICK REGAL 3.8 TURBO 3791 cm^3

Engine—water-cooled, V6, front mounted, bore x stroke 96.5 x 86.4, displacement 3791 cm^3, ohv compression ratio 8:1, max. power 123 kW (167 bhp) at 4000/min, max. torque 359 Nm (265 lbf.ft) at 2800/min, 1 Rochester four-barrel carburettor; exhaust driven Garett/Aikesearch turbine.
Transmission—rear wheels, GM. automatic transmission.
Steering—recirculating ball, servo-assisted.
Suspension—front/rear independent wishbones with anti-roll bar, dead axle with anti-roll bar.
Springs—coil springs and telescopic shock absorbers front and rear.
Brakes—front/rear   discs/drums, servo-assisted.
Dimensions and weights—length 5070mm, width 1830mm, height 1360mm, wheelbase 2745mm, kerb weight 1595 kg
Tyres—185 HR 14.
Capacities—engine sump 4.7 litres (8.25 Imp. pints), cooling system 12.4 litres (21.75 Imp. pints), fuel tank 68.5 litres (15 Imp. gal).
  Notes—Top speed 181 km/h (112 mph)

CADILLAC SEVILLE 5737 cm^3

Engine—water-cooled, V8, front mounted, bore x stroke 103.05 x 85.98, displacement 5737 cm^3, ohv, compression ratio 8:1, max. power 126 kW (171 bhp) at 4200/min, max. torque 366 Nm (270 lbf.ft) at 2000/min, Bendix electronic fuel injection.
Transmission—rear wheels, GM. automatic transmission.
Steering—recirculating ball, servo-assisted.
Suspension—front/rear independent wishbones with anti-roll bar, dead axle.
Springs—front coil springs, rear leaf springs, telescopic shock absorbers front and rear with rear automatic levelling control.
Brakes—front/rear discs, servo-assisted.
Dimensions and weights—length 5180mm, width 1825 mm, height 1390mm, wheelbase 2905mm, kerb weight 1950 kg.
Tyres—GR 78 x 15.
Capacities—engine sump 4.7 litres (8.25 Imp. pints), cooling system 16.3 litres (28.75 Imp. pints), fuel tank 79.5 litres (17.50 Imp. gal).
Notes—Top speed 185 km/h (115 mph).

CHEVROLET MALIBU CLASSIC   4998 cm^3

Engine—water-cooled, V8, front mounted, bore x stroke 94.9 x 88.3, displacement 4998 cm^3, ohv, compression ratio 8.4:1, max. power 107 kW (145 bhp) at 3800/min, max. torque 331 Nm (244 lbf.ft) at 2400/min, 1 Rochester double carburettor.
Transmission—rear wheels, automatic transmission.
Steering—recirculating ball, servo-assisted.
Suspension—front/rear independent wishbones with anti-roll bar, dead axle.
Springs—coil springs and telescopic ahsock absorbers front and rear.
Brakes—front/rear discs/drums, servo-assisted.
Dimensions and weights—length 4890mm, width 1820mm height 1380mm, wheelbase 2750mm, kerb weight 1500kg.
Tyres—P 205/70 R 14.
Capacities—engine sump 4.0 litres (7 Imp. pints), cooling system 18.1 litres (32 Imp. pints), fuel tank 66 litres (14.50 Imp. gal).
    Notes—Top speed 170 km/h. (105 mph).

1979

CHEVROLET CORVETTE   5728 cm^3

Engine—water-cooled, V8 cylinder, front mounted, bore x stroke 101.6 x 88.36, displacement 5728 cm^3, ohv, compression ratio 8.2:1, max. power 136 kW (185 bhp) at 4000/min, max. torque 353 Nm (261 lbf.ft) at 3600/min, 1 Rochester double carburettor.
Transmission—rear wheels; automatic transmission.
Steering—recirculating ball, servo-assisted.
Suspension—front/rear independent wishbones with anti-roll bar.
Springs—front coil springs, rear transversal leaf springs, telescopic shock absorbers front and rear.
Brakes—front/rear discs, servo-assisted.
Dimensions and weights—length 4704mm, width 1753mm height 1219mm, wheelbase 2489mm, kerb weight 1562kg.
Tyres—225/70 VR 15.
Capacities—engine sump 4.7 litres (8.25 Imp. pints), cooling system 20.4 litres (36 Imp. pints), fuel tank 91 litres (20 Imp. gal).
  Notes—Top speed 200 km/h. (124 mph).

CHRYSLER LEBARON MEDAILLON 5210 cm^3

Engine—water-cooled, V-8-cylinder, front mounted, bore x stroke 99.31 x 84.07, displacement 5210 cm^3, ohv, compression ratio 8.5:1, max. power 114 kW (155 bhp) at 4000/min, max. torque 388 Nm (286 lbf.ft) at 1600/min, 1 Carter double carburettor.
Transmission—rear wheels, Chrysler automatic transmission.
Steering—recirculating ball, servo-assisted.
Suspension—front/rear independent wishbones with anti-roll bar, dead axle.
Springs—front transversal torsion bars, rear transversal leaf springs, telescopic shock absorbers front and rear.
Brakes—front/rear discs/drums, servo-assisted.
Dimensions and weights—length 5240mm, width 1850 mm, height 1405mm, wheelbase 2860mm, kerb weight 1750 kg.
Tyres—GR 78-15.
Capacities—engine sump 4.7 litres (8.25 Imp. pints), cooling system 15.1 litres (26.50 Imp. pints), fuel tank 74 litres (16.25 Imp. gal).
  Notes—Top speed 170 km/h (105 mph).

CHRYSLER SUNBEAM 1300 GL   1295 cm^3

Engine—water-cooled, 4-cylinder, in-line, front mounted, bore x stroke 78.6 x 66.7, displacement 1295 cm^3, ohv, compression ratio 8.8:1, max. power 43 kW (58 bhp) at 5000/min, max. torque 93 Nm (69 lbf.ft) at 2600/min. 1 Zenith/Stromberg single carburettor.
Transmission—rear wheels; 4-speed gearbox.
Steering—rack and pinion.
Suspension—front/rear McPherson struts with anti-roll bar, dead axle with Panhard rod.
Springs—coil springs and telescopic shock absorbers front and rear.
Brakes—front/rear discs/drums, servo-assisted.
Dimensions and weights—length 3830mm, width 1600 mm, height 1390mm, wheelbase 2410mm, kerb weight 885 kg.
Tyres—155 SR 13.
Capacities—engine sump, 4 litres (7 Imp. pints). cooling system 7.3 litres (12.75 Imp. pints), fuel tank 41 litres (9 Imp. gal).
   Notes—Top speed 144 km/h (89 mph)

CHRYSLER 2-LITRES 1981 cm^3

Engine—water-cooled, 4-cylinder, in-line, front mounted,
bore x stroke 91.7 x 75, displacement 1981 cm^3, ohc,
compression ratio 9.45:1, max. power 81 kW (110 bhp)
at 5800/min, max. torque 163 Nm (120 lbf.ft) at 3400/
min, 1 Weber carburettor.
Transmission—rear wheels; 4-speed gearbox.
Steering—rack and pinion.
Suspension—front/rear McPherson struts with anti-roll
bar, dead axle.
Springs—coil springs and telescopic shock absorbers front
and rear.
Brakes—front/rear discs, servo-assisted.
Dimensions and weights—length 4527mm, width 1728
mm, height 1448mm, wheelbase 2667mm, kerb weight
1125 kg.
Tyres—175 HR 14.
Capacities—engine sump 4 litres (7 Imp. pints),
cooling system 10 litres (17.50 Imp. pints), fuel tank
65 litres (14.25 Imp. gal).
   Notes—Top speed 167 km/h (104 mph).

CHRYSLER (FRANCE) HORIZON LS

1118 cm^3

Engine—water-cooled, 4-cylinder, in-line, front mounted,
bore x stroke 74 x 65, displacement 1118 cm^3, ohv,
compression ratio 9.6 1, max. power 43.4 kW (58 bhp)
at 5600/min, max. torque 91 Nm (67 lbf.ft) at 3000/min,
1 Solex single carburettor.
Transmission—front wheels; 4-speed gearbox.
Steering—rack and pinion.
Suspension—front/rear independent wishbones with anti-
roll bar, independent trailing arms.
Springs—front: longitudinal torsion bars, rear: coil springs,
telescopic shock absorbers front and rear.
Brakes—front/rear discs/drums, servo-assisted.
Dimensions and weights—length 3960mm, width 1680mm
height 1410mm, wheelbase 2520mm, kerb weight 960 kg.
Tyres—145 SR 13.
Capacities—engine sump 3.3 litres (5.75 Imp. pints),
cooling system 6 litres (10.50 Imp. pints), fuel tank
47 litres (21.25 Imp. gal).
  Notes—Top speed 148 km/h (92 mph).

CITROEN 2 CV 6   602 cm^3

Engine—air-cooled 2-cylinder, flat engine, front mounted,
bore x stroke 74 x 70, displacement 602 cm^3, ohv,
compression ratio 8.5:1, max. power 19 kW (26 bhp) at
5500/min, max. torque 39 Nm (29 lbf.ft) at 3500/min.
1 Solex single carburettor.
Transmission—front wheels; 4-speed gearbox.
Steering—rack and pinion.
Suspension—front/rear independent wishbones,
independent longitudinal trailing arms.
Springs—Telescopic shock absorbers and longitudinal
coil springs linking front and rear.
Brakes—front/rear drums, servo-assisted.
Dimensions and weights—length 3830mm, width 1480mm,
height 1600mm, wheelbase 2400mm, kerb weight 560 kg.
Tyres—125 - 15 X.
Capacities—engine sump 2.5 litres (4.50 Imp. pints),
fuel tank 20 litres (4.50 Imp. gal).

  Notes—Top speed 110 km/h (68 mph)

CITROEN ACADIANE
602 cm^3

Engine—air-cooled, 2-cylinder, flat engine, front mounted, bore x stroke 70 x 74, displacement 602 cm^3, ohv, compression ratio 8.5:1, max. power 23 kW (31 bhp) at 5750min, max. torque 41 Nm (30 lbf.ft) at 3500/min, 1 Solex carburettor.
Transmission—front wheels; 4-speed gearbox.
Steering—rack and pinion.
Suspension—front/rear independent wishbones, independent trailing arms.
Springs—longitudinal coil springs and telescopic shock absorbers front and rear.
Brakes—front/rear discs/drums.
Dimensions and weights—length 4030mm, width 1500 mm height 1825mm, wheelbase 2535mm, kerb weight 680 kg.
Tyres—135-15 X.
Capacities—engine sump 2.5 litres (4.50 Imp. pints), fuel tank 25 litres (5.50 Imp. gal).
 Notes—Top speed 100 km/h (62 mph).

CITROEN LN   602 cm^3

Engine—air-cooled, 2-cylinder, flat engine, front mounted
bore x stroke 74 x 70, displacement 602 cm^3, ohv,
compression ratio 9:1, max. power 24 kW (33 bhp) at
5750/min, max. torque 41 Nm (30 lbf.ft) at 3500/min.
1 Solex carburettor.
Transmission—front wheels; 4-speed gearbox.
Steering—rack and pinion.
Suspension—front/rear McPherson struts with anti-roll
bar, independent trailing arms.
Springs—coil springs and telescopic shock absorbers front
and rear.
Brakes—front/rear discs/drums.
Dimensions and weights—length 3386mm, width 1522mm,
height 1373mm, wheelbase 2230mm, kerb weight 706 kg.
Tyres—135 SR 13.
Capacities—engine sump 2.1 litres (3.75 Imp. pints),
fuel tank 40 litres (8.75 Imp. gal).
  Notes—Top speed 120 km/h (74 mph)

CITROEN VISA SUPER

1124 cm^3

Engine—water-cooled, 4-cylinder, in-line, front mounted, bore x stroke 72 x 69, displacement 1124 cm^3, ohc, compression ratio 9.2:1, max. power 41 Kw (56 bhp) at 6250/min, max. torque 79 Nm (58 lbf.ft) at 3000/min. 1 Solex double carburettor.
Transmission—front wheels; 4-speed gearbox.
Steering—rack and pinion.
Suspension—front/rear McPherson struts with anti-roll bar, independent trailing arms.
Springs—coil springs and telescopic shock absorbers front and rear.
Brakes—front/rear discs/drums, servo-assisted.
Dimensions and weights—length 3690mm, width 1534mm height 1415, wheelbase 2420mm, kerb weight 800 kg.
Tyres—145 SR 13 XZX
Capacities—engine sump 4.5 litres (8 Imp. pints), cooling system 5.5 litres (9.75 Imp. pints), fuel tank 40 litres (8.75 Imp. gal).

　Notes—Top speed 144 km/h (89 mph)

CITROEN G SPECIAL   1129 cm^3

Engine—air-cooled, 4-cylinder, flat engine, front mounted,
bore x stroke 74 x 65.6, displacement 1129 cm^3, 2 x ohc,
compression ratio 9:1, max. power 40 kW (54 bhp) at
5750/min, max. torque 78 Nm (61 lbf.ft) at 3500/min,
1 Solex or Weber carburettor.
Transmission—front wheels; 4-speed gearbox.
Steering—rack and pinion.
Suspension—front/rear independent wishbones with anti-
roll bar, independent trailing arms.
Springs—hydro-pneumatic system front and rear with
automatic levelling control.
Brakes—front/rear discs, servo-assisted.
Dimensions and weights—length 4120mm, width 1608
mm, height 1349mm, wheelbase 2550mm, kerb weight
925 kg.
Tyres—145 SR 15.
Capacities—engine sump 4 litres (7 Imp. pints), fuel tank
43 litres (9.50 Imp. gal). GS Pallas illustrated.
  Notes—Top speed 149 km/h (92 mph).

CITROEN GS X3

1299 cm^3

Engine—air-cooled, 4-cylinder, flat engine, front mounted, bore x stroke 74 x 65.6, displacement 1299 cm^3, 2 x ohc compression ratio 8.7:1, max. power 48 kW (65 bhp) at 5500/min, max. torque 98 Nm (72 lbf.ft) at 3500/min, 1 Solex or Weber carburettor.
Transmission—front wheels; 4-speed gearbox.
Steering—rack and pinion.
Suspension—front/rear independent wishbones with anti-roll bar, independent trailing arms.
Springs—hydro-pneumatic system front and rear with automatic levelling control.
Brakes—front/rear discs, servo-assisted.
Dimensions and weights—length 4120mm, width 1608mm height 1349mm, wheelbase 2550mm, kerb weight 940 kg.
Tyres—145 SR 15 XZX.
Capacities—engine sump 4 litres (7 Imp. pints), fuel tank 43 litres (9.50 Imp. gal).
Notes—Top speed 158 km/h (98 mph).

CITROEN CX 2000   1985 cm^3

Engine—water-cooled, 4-cylinder, in-line, front mounted, bore x stroke 86 x 85.5, displacement 1985 cm^3, ohv, compression ratio 9:1, max. power 74 kW (101 bhp) at 5500/min, max. torque 149 Nm (110 lbf.ft) at 3000/min 1 Weber carburettor.
Transmission—front wheels; 4-speed gearbox.
Steering—rack and pinion.
Suspension—front/rear independent wishbones with anti-roll bar, independent trailing arms.
Springs—hydro-pneumatic system front and rear, automatic levelling control.
Brakes—front/rear discs, servo-assisted.
Dimensions and weights—length 4666mm, width 1734 mm, height 1360mm, wheelbase 2845mm, kerb weight 1265 kg.
Tyres—front: 185 SR 14 ZX, rear: 175 SR 14 ZX.
Capacities—engine sump 5.3 litres (9.25 Imp. pints), cooling system 10.6 litres (18.75 Imp. pints), fuel tank 68 litres (15 Imp. gal).
  Notes—Top speed 174 km/h (108 mph).

CITROEN CX 2500 D

2500 cm^3

Engine—water-cooled, 4-cylinder, diesel, front mounted, bore x stroke 93 x 92, displacement 2500 cm^3 ohv, compression ratio 22,25:1, max. power 55 kW (75 bhp) at 4250/min, max. torque 150 Nm (111 lbf.ft) at 2000/min, fuel-injection Bosch or Rotodiesel.
Transmission—front wheels, 4-speed gearbox.
Steering—rack and pinion.
Suspension—front/rear independent wishbones with anti-roll bar, independent trailing arms.
Springs—Hydro pneumatic system front and rear. Automatic levelling control.
Brakes—front/rear discs, servo-assisted.
Dimensions and weights—length 4660mm, width 1730mm, height 1360mm, wheelbase 2845mm, kerb weight 1350kg.
Tyres—front: 185 SR 14 ZX, rear: 175 SR 14 ZX.
Capacities—engine sump 5.8 litres (10.25 Imp. pints), cooling system 12.3 litres (21.50 Imp. pints), fuel tank 68 litres (15 Imp. gal).

  Notes—Top speed 147 km/h (91 mph)

DACIA 1300 L 1289 cm^3

Engine—water-cooled, 4-cylinder, in-line, front mounted, bore x stroke 73 x 77, displacement 1289 cm^3, ohv, compression ratio 8.5:1, max. power 40 kW (54 bhp) at 5250/min, max. torque 95 Nm (70 lbf.ft) at 3500/min. 1 Carfil single carburettor.
Transmission—front wheels; 4-speed gearbox.
Steering—rack and pinion.
Suspension—front/rear independent wishbones with anti-roll bar. Dead axle.
Springs—coil springs and telescopic shock absorbers front and rear.
Brakes—front/rear discs/drums, servo-assisted.
Dimensions and weights—length 4348mm, width 1616mm height 1435mm, wheelbase 2441mm, kerb weight 900 kg.
Tyres—155 SR 13.
Capacities—engine sump 3 litres (5.25 Imp. pints), cooling system 5 litres (8.75 Imp. pints), fuel tank 47 litres (10.25 Imp. gal).

Notes—Top speed 145 km/h (90 mph)

DAIHATSU CHARADE XTE 993 cm^3

Engine—water-cooled, 3-cylinder, in-line, front mounted, bore x stroke 76 x 73, displacement 993 cm^3, ohc, compression ratio 8.7:1, max. power 41 kW (56 bhp) at 5500/min, max. torque 77 Nm (57 lbf.ft) at 2800/min. 1 Aisan/Stromberg carburettor.
Transmission—front wheels; 5-speed gearbox.
Steering—rack and pinion.
Suspension—front/rear McPherson struts, dead axle with Panhard rod.
Springs—coil springs and telescopic shock absorbers front and rear.
Brakes—front/rear discs/drums, servo-assisted.
Dimensions and weights—length 3485mm, width 1510mm height 1360mm, wheelbase 2300mm, kerb weight 660 kg.
Tyres—155 SR 12.
Capacities—engine sump 2.9 litres (5 Imp. pints), cooling system 4 litres (7 Imp. pints), fuel tank 34 litres (7.50 Imp. gal).
  Notes—Top speed 140 km/h (87 mph)

DAIHATSU CHARMANT 1400 SEDAN 1407 cm^3

Engine—water-cooled, 4-cylinder, in-line, front mounted,
bore x stroke 80 x 70, displacement 1407 cm^3, ohv,
compression ratio 8.5:1, max. power 63 kW (86 bhp) at
6000/min, max. torque 118 Nm (87 lbf.ft) at 3800/min.
1 Aisan single carburettor.
Transmission—rear wheels; 4-speed gearbox.
Steering—recirculating ball.
Suspension—front/rear McPherson struts, dead axle.
Springs—front coil springs, rear transversal leaf springs,
telescopic shock absorbers front and rear.
Brakes—front/rear discs/drums, servo-assisted.
Dimensions and weights—length 4000 mm, width 1520mm
height 1370mm, wheelbase 2335mm, kerb weight 885 kg.
Tyres—155 SK 13.
Capacities—engine sump 4.4 litres (7.75 Imp. pints),
cooling system 7 litres (12.25 Imp. pints), fuel tank
43 litres (9.50 Imp. gal).
  Notes—Top speed 150 km/h (93 mph)

DAIMLER DOUBLE-SIX 5343 cm^3

Engine—water-cooled, 12-cylinder, front mounted, bore x stroke 90 x 70, displacement 5343 cm^3, 2 x ohc, compression ratio 9:1, max. power 209 kW (284 bhp) at 5750/min, max. torque 399 Nm (294 lbf.ft) at 3500/min. fuel injection Bosch-Lucas D-Jetronic.
Transmission—rear wheels; automatic transmission Turbo-Hydramatic.
Steering—rack and pinion, servo-assisted.
Suspension—front/rear independent wishbones with anti-roll bar, independent trailing arms.
Springs—coil springs and telescopic shock absorbers front and rear.
Brakes—front/rear discs, servo-assisted.
Dimensions and weights—length 4945mm, width 1770mm height 1375mm, wheelbase 2865mm, kerb weight 1885kg.
Tyres—205/70 VR 15.
Capacities—engine sump 10.8 litres (19 Imp pints, cooling system 20.5 litres (36 Imp. pints), fuel tank 91 litres (20 Imp. gal).
  Notes—Top speed 225 km/h (140 mph)

DATSUN SUNNY 1400GL

$1397cm^3$

Engine—water-cooled, 4-cylinder, in-line, front mounted, bore x stroke 76 x 77, displacement 1397 cm^3, ohv, compression ratio 9:1, max. power 59 kW (80 bhp) at 6000/min, max. torque 113 Nm (83 lbf.ft) at 3600/min, 1 Hitachi carburettor.

Transmission—rear wheels; 4-speed gearbox.

Steering—recirculating ball.

Suspension—front/rear McPherson struts, dead axle.

Springs—coil springs and telescopic shock absorbers front and rear.

Brakes—front/rear discs/drums.

Dimensions and weights—length 3940, USA 4140mm, width 1580mm, height 1360mm, wheelbase 2340mm, kerb weight 850 kg.

Tyres—155 SR 13.

Capacities—engine sump 3.4 litres (6 Imp. pints), cooling system 4.1 litres (7.25 Imp. pints), fuel tank 50 litres (11 Imp. gal).

   Notes—USA version: compression ratio 8.5:1, 52 kW at 6000/min, 102 Nm at 3600/min.

   Notes—Top speed 155 km/h (96 mph)

DATSUN VIOLET COUPE

1595 cm^3

Engine—water-cooled, 4-cylinder, in-line, front mounted, bore x stroke 83 x 73.7, displacement 1595 cm^3, 1 ohc, compression ratio 9:1, max. power 64 kW (87 bhp) at 5800/min, max. torque 124 Nm (92 lbf.ft) at 3800/min, 2 SU carburettors.

Transmission—rear wheels; 5-speed gearbox.

Steering—recirculating ball.

Suspension—front/rear McPherson struts with anti-roll bar, dead axle.

Springs—coil springs and telescopic shock absorbers front and rear.

Brakes—front/rear discs/drums, servo-assisted.

Dimensions and weights—length 4080mm, width 1600mm height 1350mm, wheelbase 2400mm, kerb weight 960 kg.

Tyres—165 SR 13.

Capacities—engine sump 4.3 litres (7.50 Imp. pints), cooling system 6.3 litres (11 Imp. pints), fuel tank 50 litres (11 Imp. gal).

Notes—Top speed 165 km/h (102 mph)

DATSUN 180 BLUEBIRD
HARDTOP SSS
$1770\ cm^3$

Engine—water-cooled, 4-cylinder, in-line, front mounted, bore x stroke 85 x 78, displacement $1770\ cm^3$, 1 ohc, compression ratio 8.5:1, max. power 66 kW (90 bhp) at 5800/min, max. torque 136 Nm (100 lbf.ft) at 3800/min 2 SU carburettors.

Transmission—rear wheels; 5-speed gearbox.

Steering—recirculating ball.

Suspension—front/rear McPherson struts with anti-roll bar, independent trailing arms.

Springs—coil springs and telescopic shock absorbers front and rear.

Brakes—front/rear discs/drums, servo-assisted.

Dimensions and weights—length 4260mm, width 1630 mm, height 1380mm, wheelbase 2500mm, kerb weight 1060 kg.

Tyres—185/70 HR 14.

Capacities—engine sump 4.3 litres (7.50 Imp. pints), cooling system 6.8 litres (12 Imp. pints), fuel tank 60 litres (13.25 Imp. gal).

   Notes—Top speed 170 km/h (105 mph)

DATSUN LAUREL

1998 cm^3

Engine—water-cooled, 6-cylinder, in-line, front mounted, bore x stroke 78 x 69.7, displacement 1998 cm^3, 1 ohc, compression ratio 8.6:1, max. power 71 kW (97 bhp) at 5600/min, max. torque 135 Nm (100 lbf.ft) at 3600/min, 1 Hitachi carburettor.

Transmission—rear wheels; 4-speed gearbox.

Steering—recirculating ball.

Suspension—front/rear McPherson struts with anti-roll bar, dead axle.

Springs—coil springs and telescopic shock absorbers front and rear.

Brakes—front/rear discs/drums, servo-assisted.

Dimensions and weights—length 4530mm, width 1690mm height 1400mm, wheelbase 2670mm, kerb weight 1170kg.

Tyres—185/70 SR 14.

Capacities—engine sump 5.7 litres (10 Imp. pints), cooling system 8.2 litres (14.50 Imp. pints), fuel tank 60 litres (13.25 Imp. gal).

  Notes—Top speed 165 km/h (102 mph)

DATSUN 260C 2565 cm^3

Engine—water-cooled, 6-cylinder, in-line, front mounted,
bore x stroke 83 x 79, displacement 2565 cm^3, 1 ohc,
compression ratio 8.3:1, max. power 87 kW (118 bhp) at
5200/min, max. torque 179 Nm (132 lbf.ft) at 3200/min,
1 Hitachi carburettor.
Transmission—rear wheels; Nissan. automatic transmission.
Steering—recirculating ball, servo-assisted.
Suspension—front/rear independent wishbones with anti-
roll bar, dead axle with anti-roll bar.
Springs—front coil springs, rear transversal leaf springs,
telescopic shock absorbers front and rear.
Brakes—front/rear discs/drums, servo-assisted.
Dimensions and weights—length 4690mm, width 1690mm
height 1440mm, wheelbase 2690mm, kerb weight 1420kg.
Tyres—195/70 HR 14.
Capacities—engine sump 4.7 litres (8.25 Imp. pints),
cooling system 9 litres (16 Imp. pints), fuel tank 67
litres (14. 75 Imp. gal).

   Notes—Top speed 160 km/h (99 mph)

DATSUN 260Z 2+2

2565 cm^3

Engine—water-cooled, 6-cylinder, in-line, front mounted, bore x stroke 83 x 79, displacement 2565 cm^3, 1 ohc, compression ratio 8.3:1, max. power 110 kW (150 bhp) at 5600/min, max. torque 215 Nm (159 lbf.ft) at 4400/min. 2 SU carburettors.
Transmission—rear wheels; 5-speed gearbox.
Steering—rack and pinion.
Suspension—front/rear McPherson struts with anti-roll bar, independent trailing arms.
Springs—coil springs and telescopic shock absorbers front and rear.
Brakes—front/rear discs/drums, servo-assisted.
Dimensions and weights—length 4425mm, width 1650mm, height 1295mm, wheelbase 2605mm, kerb weight 1200 kg.
Tyres—195/70 VR 14.
Capacities—engine sump 4.7 litres (8.25 Imp. pints), cooling system 9.7 litres (17 Imp. pints), fuel tank 65 litres (14.25 Imp. gal).
   Notes—Top speed 195 km/h (121 mph)

De TOMASO LONGCHAMP   5763 cm³

Engine—water-cooled, V-8, front mounted, bore x stroke
101.65 × 88.9, displacement 5763 cm³, ohv, compression
ratio 8.5:1, max. power 199 kW (271 bhp) at 5000/min,
max. torque 434 Nm (320 lbf.ft) at 3500/min, 1 Motor-
craft carburettor.
Transmission—rear wheels; automatic transmission.
Steering—rack and pinion, servo-assisted.
Suspension—front/rear independent wishbones with anti-
roll bar, independent trailing arms.
Springs—coil springs and telescopic shock absorbers front
and rear.
Brakes—front/rear discs, servo-assisted.
Dimensions and weights—length 4530mm, width 1830mm
height 1295mm, wheelbase 2600mm, kerb weight 1700kg.
Tyres—215/70 VR15.
Capacities—engine sump 5.5 litres (9.75 Imp. pints),
cooling system 18 litres (31.75 Imp. pints), fuel tanks
100 litres (22 Imp. gal).
  Notes—Top speed 240 km/h (149 mph).

DODGE ASPEN COUPE   5211 cm^3

Engine—water-cooled, V8 cylinder, front mounted, bore
x stroke 99.3 x 84, displacement 5211 cm^3, ohv,
compression ratio 8.4:1, max. power 103 kW (140 bhp)
at 4000/min, max. torque 331 Nm (244 lbf.ft) at 1600/
min, 1 Carter double carburettor.
Transmission—rear wheels; Chrysler. automatic
transmission.
Steering—recirculating ball, servo-assisted.
Suspension—front/rear struts, independent wishbones
with anti-roll bar, dead axle.
Springs—front torsion bars, rear leaf springs, telescopic
shock absorbers front and rear.
Brakes—front/rear discs/drums, servo-assisted.
Dimensions and weights—length 5110mm, width 1860mm
height 1400mm, wheelbase 2860mm, kerb weight 1575kg.
Tyres—D 78 x 14.
Capacities—engine sump 4.7 litres (8.25 Imp. pints),
cooling system 15.1 litres (26.50 Imp. pints), fuel tank
68 litres (15 Imp. gal).
   Notes—Top speed 170 km/h (105 mph)

FERRARI 400 GT/4

4823 cm^3

Engine—water-cooled, V12, front mounted, bore x stroke
81 x 78, displacement 4823 cm^3, 2 x 2 ohc, compression
ratio 8.8:1, max. power 250 kW (340 bhp) at 6500/min,
max. torque 471 Nm (348 lbf.ft) at 3600/min, 6 Weber
double carburettors.
Transmission—rear wheels; automatic transmission Turbo
/Hydramatic.
Steering—worm and roller, servo-assisted.
Suspension—front/rear independent wishbones with anti-
roll bar, independent trailing arms.
Springs—coil springs and telescopic shock absorbers front
and rear.
Brakes—front/rear discs, servo-assisted.
Dimensions and weights—length 4810mm, width 1800mm
height 1310mm, wheelbase 2700mm, kerb weight 1880kg.
Tyres—215/70 VR 15 X.
Capacities—engine sump 18.5 litres (32.50 Imp. pints),
cooling system 20 litres (35.25 Imp. pints), fuel tank
110 litres (24.25 Imp. gal).

   Notes—Top speed 240 km/h (149 mph)

FERRARI BB 512

4942 cm^3

Engine—water-cooled, 12-cylinder, flat engine, centre mounted, bore x stroke 82 x 78, displacement 4942 cm^3 2 ohc, compression ratio 9.2:1, max. power 265 kW (360 bhp) at 6800/min, max. torque 451 Nm (333 lbf.ft) at 4600/min, 4 Weber three-barrel carburettors.
Transmission—rear wheels; 5-speed gearbox.
Steering—rack and pinion, servo-assisted.
Suspension—front/rear independent wishbones with anti-roll bar, independent wishbones with anti-roll bar.
Springs—coil springs and telescopic shock absorbers front and rear.
Brakes—front/rear discs, servo-assisted.
Dimensions and weights—length 4400mm, width 1830mm height 1120mm, wheelbase 2500mm, kerb weight 1515kg.
Tyres—front: 215/70 VR 15, rear: 225/70 VR 15.
Capacities—engine sump $\pm$ 18 litres (31.75 Imp. pints), cooling system 20 litres (35.25 Imp. pints), fuel tank 110 litres (24.25 Imp. gal).

  Notes—Top speed 290 km/h (180 mph)

FIAT 126 PERSONAL 4   652 cm³

Engine—air-cooled, 2-cylinder, in-line, rear mounted,
bore x stroke 77 x 70, displacement 652 cm³, ohv,
compression ratio 7.5:1, max. power 18 kW (24 bhp) at
4500/min, max. torque 41 Nm (30 lbf.ft) at 3000/min.
1 Weber single carburettor.
Transmission—rear wheels; 4-speed gearbox.
Steering—worm and roller.
Suspension—front/rear independent wishbones,
independent trailing arms.
Springs—front transversal leaf springs, rear coil springs
and telescopic shock absorbers, front and rear.
Brakes—front/rear drums.
Dimensions and weights—length 3129mm, width 1382mm
height 1335mm, wheelbase 1840mm, kerb weight 600 kg.
Tyres—135 SR12.
Capacities—engine sump 2.5 litres (4.50 Imp. pints),
fuel tank 21 litres (4.50 Imp. gal.).

   Notes—Top speed 105 km/h (65 mph)

FIAT 127 1050CL

1049 cm^3

Engine—water-cooled, 4-cylinder, in-line, front mounted, bore x stroke 76 x 57.8, displacement 1049 cm^3, ohc, compression ratio 9.3:1, max. power 37 kW (50 bhp) at 5600/min, max. torque 77 Nm (57 lbf.ft) at 4000/min, Weber/Solex single carburettor.

Transmission—front wheels; 4-speed gearbox.

Steering—rack and pinion.

Suspension—McPherson struts.

Springs—front coil springs, rear transversal leaf spring and telescopic shock absorbers front and rear.

Brakes—front/rear discs/drums.

Dimensions and weights—length 3645mm, width 1527mm height 1358mm, wheelbase 2225mm, kerb weight 730 kg.

Tyres—135 SR 13.

Capacities—engine sump 3.1 litres (5.50 Imp. pints), cooling system 5.5 litres (9.75 Imp. pints), fuel tank 30 litres (6.50 Imp. gal).

   Notes—Top speed 140 km/h (87 mph)

FIAT 128 1100 CL 1116 cm^3

Engine—water-cooled, 4-cylinder, in-line, front mounted, bore x stroke 80 x 55.5, displacement 1116 cm^3, ohc, compression ratio 9.2:1, max. power 40 kW (54 bhp) at 6000/min, max. torque 81 Nm (60 lbf.ft) at 2800/min, 1 Weber/Solex single carburettor.
Transmission—front wheels; 4-speed gearbox.
Steering—rack and pinion.
Suspension—McPherson struts.
Springs—front coil springs, rear transversal leaf spring and telescopic shock absorbers front and rear.
Brakes—front/rear discs/drums, servo-assisted.
Dimensions and weights—length 3840mm, width 1590mm height 1420mm, wheelbase 2448mm, kerb weight 770 kg.
Tyres—145 SR13.
Capacities—engine sump 4.3 litres (7.50 Imp. pints), cooling system 6.5 litres (11.50 Imp. pints), fuel tank 38 litres (8.25 Imp. gal).
  Notes—Top speed 140 km/h (87 mph)

FIAT RITMO 65 CL   1301 cm^3

Engine—water-cooled, 4-cylinder, in-line, front mounted,
bore x stroke 86.4 x 55.5, displacement 1301 cm^3, ohc,
compression ratio 9.1:1, max. power 48 kW (65 bhp) at
5800/min, max. torque 98 Nm (72 lbf.ft) at 3500/min,
1 Weber or Solex single carburettor.
Transmission—front wheels; 5-speed gearbox.
Steering—rack and pinion.
Suspension—front/rear McPherson struts, independent
trailing arms.
Springs—coil springs and telescopic shock absorbers front
and rear.
Brakes—front/rear discs/drums, servo-assisted.
Dimensions and weights—length 3937mm, width 1650mm
height 1400mm, wheelbase 2448mm, kerb weight 895 kg.
Tyres—145 SR 13
Capacities—engine sump 4.7 litres (8.25 Imp. pints),
cooling system 7.9 litres (14 Imp. pints), fuel tank
51 litres (11.25 Imp. gal).

  Notes—Top speed 150 km/h (93 mph)

FIAT 124D-1200   1197 cm^3

Engine—water-cooled, 4-cylinder, in-line, front mounted, bore x stroke 73 x 71.5, displacement 1197 cm^3, ohv, compression ratio 8.8:1, max. power 48 kW (65 bhp) at 5600/min, max. torque 88 Nm (65 lbf.ft) at 3700/min, 1 Bressel carburettor.
Transmission—rear wheels; 4-speed gearbox.
Steering—worm and roller.
Suspension—front/rear independent wishbones with anti-roll bar, dead axle.
Springs—coil springs and telescopic shock absorbers front and rear.
Brakes—front/rear discs, servo-assisted.
Dimensions and weights—length 4042mm, width 1611 mm, height 1420mm, wheelbase 2420mm, kerb weight 905 kg.
Tyres—155 SR 13.
Capacities—engine sump 3.9 litres (6.75 Imp. pints), cooling system 7.5 litres (13.25 Imp. pints), fuel tank 39 litres (8.50 Imp. gal).
  Notes—Top speed 140 km/h (87 mph).

FIAT 131 MIRAFIORI 1300 1297 cm^3

Engine—water-cooled, 4-cylinder, in-line, front mounted, bore x stroke 76 x 71.5, displacement 1297 cm^3, ohv, compression ratio 9.2:1, max. power 55 kW (75 bhp) at 5200/min, max. torque 124 Nm (92 lbf.ft) at 3000/min 1 Weber/Solex double carburettor.
Transmission—rear wheels; 4-speed gearbox.
Steering—rack and pinion.
Suspension—front/rear McPherson struts, dead axle with Panhard rod.
Springs—coil springs and telescopic shock absorbers front and rear.
Brakes—front/rear discs/drums, servo-assisted.
Dimensions and weights—length 4264mm, width 1651mm, height 1381mm, wheelbase 2490mm, kerb weight 1000kg.
Tyres—155 SR 13.
Capacities—engine sump 4 litres (7 Imp. pints), cooling system 7.6 litres (13.25 Imp. pints), fuel tank 50 litres (11 Imp. gal).
  Notes—Top speed 150 km/h (93 mph)

FIAT 131 SUPERMIRAFIORI 1600TC   1585 cm^3

Engine—water-cooled, 4-cylinder, in-line, front mounted, bore x stroke 84 x 71.5, displacement 1585 cm^3, dohc, compression ratio 9:1, max. power 71 kW (97 bhp) at 6000/min, max. torque 128 Nm (94 lbf.ft) at 3800/min, 1 Weber double carburettor.
Transmission—rear wheels; 5-speed gearbox.
Steering—rack and pinion.
Suspension—front/rear McPherson struts, dead axle with Panhard rod.
Springs—coil springs and telescopic shock absorbers front and rear.
Brakes—front/rear discs/drums, servo-assisted.
Dimensions and weights—length 4231mm, width 1651mm height 1381mm, wheelbase 2490mm, kerb weight 1050 kg.
Tyres—165 SR 13.
Capacities—engine sump 4.1 litres (7.25 Imp. pints), cooling system 8 litres (14 Imp. pints), fuel tank 50 litres (11 Imp. gal).
  Notes—Top speed 170 km/h (105 mph)

FIAT 131 MIRAFIORI DIESEL 2000   1995 cm^3

Engine—water-cooled, 4-cylinder, in-line, diesel, front
mounted, bore x stroke 88 x 82, displacement 1995 cm^3
ohc, compression ratio 22:1, max. power 44 kW (60 bhp)
at 4400/min, max. torque 112 Nm (83 lbf.ft) at 2400/min
fuel-injection pump Bosch
Transmission—rear wheels; 5-speed gearbox.
Steering—rack and pinion.
Suspension—front/rear McPherson struts, dead axle with
Panhard rod.
Springs—coil springs and telescopic shock absorbers front
and rear.
Brakes—front/rear discs/drums, servo-assisted.
Dimensions and weights—length 4264mm, width 1651mm
height 1391mm, wheelbase 2490mm, kerb weight 1160kg.
Tyres—165 SR13.
Capacities—engine sump 5.5 litres (9.75 Imp. pints),
cooling system 11 litres (19.25 Imp. pints), fuel tank
50 litres (11. Imp. gal.)
   Notes—Top speed 135 km/h (84 mph)

FIAT 132 2000   1995 cm^3

Engine—water-cooled, 4-cylinder, in-line, front mounted,
bore x stroke 84 x 90, displacement 1995 cm^3, dohc,
compression ratio 8.9:1, max. power 83 kW (113 bhp) at
5300/min, max. torque 158 Nm (117 lbf.ft) at 3000/min
Weber/Solex double carburettor.
Transmission—rear wheels; 5-speed gearbox.
Steering—worm and roller, servo-assisted.
Suspension—front/rear struts, independent wishbones
with anti-roll bar, dead axle.
Springs—coil springs and telescopic shock absorbers front
and rear.
Brakes—front/rear discs/drums, servo-assisted.
Dimensions and weights—length 4392mm, width 1640mm
height 1435mm, wheelbase 2557mm, kerb weight 1140kg.
Tyres—175/70 SR14.
Capacities—engine sump 4.1 litres (7.25 Imp. pints),
cooling system 8 litres (14 Imp. pints), fuel tank 55 litres
(12 Imp. gal).
    Notes—Top speed 170 km/h (105 mph)

FIAT 132 2500 DIESEL   2445 cm^3

Engine—water-cooled, 4-cylinder, in-line, diesel, front
mounted, bore x stroke 93 x 90, displacement 2445 cm^3
1 x ohc, compression ratio 22:1, max. power 53 kW (72
bhp) at 4200/min, max. torque 147 Nm (108 lbf.ft) at
2400/min, fuel-injection pump Bosch.
Transmission—rear wheels; 5-speed gearbox.
Steering—worm and roller, servo-assisted.
Suspension—front/rear struts, independent wishbones
with anti-roll bar independent trailing arms. dead axle.
Springs—coil springs and telescopic shock absorbers front
and rear.
Brakes—front/rear discs/drums, servo-assisted.
Dimensions and weights—length 4392mm, width 1640mm
height 1435mm, wheelbase 2557mm, kerb weight 1280kg.
Tyres—175/70 SR14.
Capacities—engine sump 5.6 litres (9.75 Imp. pints),
cooling system 11 litres (19.25 Imp. pints), fuel tank 56
litres (12.25 Imp. gal).
   Notes—Top speed 150 km/h (93 mph)

FIAT X1/9   1498 cm^3

Engine—water-cooled, 4-cylinder, in-line, centre mounted,
bore x stroke 86.4 x 63.9, displacement 1498 cm^3, ohc,
compression ratio 9.2:1, max. power 62 kW (84 bhp) at
6000/min, max. torque 118 Nm (87 lbf.ft) at 3200/min
1 Weber double carburettor.
Transmission—rear wheels, 5-speed gearbox.
Steering—rack and pinion.
Suspension—front/rear McPherson struts, independent
trailing arms.
Springs—coil springs and telescopic shock absorbers front
and rear.
Brakes—front/rear: discs/drums, servo-assisted.
Dimensions and weights—length 3969mm, width 1570mm,
height 1180mm, wheelbase 2202mm, kerb weight 920 kg.
Tyres—165/70 SR 13.
Capacities—engine sump 4.5 litres (8 Imp. pints), cooling
system 11.6 litres (20.50 Imp. pints), fuel tank 49 litres
(10.75 Imp. gal).
 Notes—Top speed 180 km/h (112 mph).

FORD FIESTA 1.1S   1117 cm^3

Engine—water-cooled, 4-cylinder, in-line, front mounted, bore x stroke 74 x 65, displacement 1117 cm^3, ohv, compression ratio 9:1, max. power 39 kW (53 bhp) at 5700/min, max. torque 80 Nm (59 lbf.ft) at 3000/min, 1 Ford carburettor.
Transmission—front wheels; 4-speed gearbox.
Steering—rack and pinion.
Suspension—front/rear McPherson struts, dead axle with Panhard rod.
Springs—coil springs and telescopic shock absorbers front and rear.
Brakes—front/rear discs/drums, servo-assisted.
Dimensions and weights—length 3565mm, width 1567 mm, height 1314mm, wheelbase 2286mm, kerb weight 745 kg.
Tyres—155 SR 12.
Capacities—engine sump 3.25 litres (5.75 Imp. pints), cooling system 5.7 litres (10 Imp. pints, fuel tank 34 litres (7.50 Imp. gal).
  Notes—Top speed 145 km/h (90 mph).

FORD ESCORT 1300L   1297 cm^3

Engine—water-cooled, 4-cylinder, in-line, front mounted, bore x stroke 80.98 x 62.99, displacement 1297 cm^3, ohv compression ratio 9.2:1, max. power 42 kW (57 bhp) at 5500/min, max. torque 91 Nm (67 lbf.ft) at 3000/min, 1 Weber carburettor.
Transmission—rear wheels; 4-speed gearbox.
Steering—rack and pinion.
Suspension—front/rear McPherson struts with anti-roll bar, dead axle.
Springs—front coil springs, rear leaf springs, telescopic shock absorbers front and rear.
Brakes—front/rear discs/drums, servo-assisted.
Dimensions and weights—length 3980mm, width 1600 mm, height 1380mm, wheelbase 2405mm, kerb weight 885 kg.
Tyres—155 SR 13.
Capacities—engine sump 3.6 litres (6.25 Imp. pints), cooling system 5 litres (8.75 Imp. pints), fuel tank 41 litres (9 Imp. gal).
   Notes—Top speed 137 km/h (85 mph).

FORD CORTINA 1600 GL   1593 cm^3

Engine—water-cooled, 4-cylinder, in-line, front mounted, bore x stroke 87.65 x 66, displacement 1593 cm^3, ohc, compression ratio 9.2:1, max. power 53 kW (72 bhp) at 5000/min, max. torque 118 Nm (87 lbf.ft) at 2700/min, 1 Ford carburettor.

Transmission—rear wheels; 4-speed gearbox.

Steering—rack and pinion.

Suspension—front/rear independent wishbones with anti-roll bar, dead axle.

Springs—coil springs and telescopic shock absorbers front and rear.

Brakes—front/rear discs/drums, servo-assisted.

Dimensions and weights—length 4330mm, width 1630 mm, height 1320mm, wheelbase 2580mm, kerb weight 1035 kg.

Tyres—165 SR 13.

Capacities—engine sump 3.75 litres (6.50 Imp. pints), cooling system 5.8 litres (10.25 Imp. pints), fuel tank 54 litres (11.75 Imp. gal).

   Notes—Top speed 152 km/h (94 mph).

FORD TAUNUS 2000 V-6 GHIA   1998cm^3

Engine—water-cooled, V-6 -cylinder, front mounted, bore x
stroke 84 x 60.1, displacement 1998 cm^3, ohv,
compression ratio 8.75:1, max. power 66 kW (90 bhp)
at 5000/min, max. torque 149 Nm (110 lbf.ft) at
3000/min, 1 Solex carburettor.
Transmission—rear wheels; 4-speed gearbox.
Steering—rack and pinion.
Suspension—front/rear independent wishbones with anti-
roll bar, dead axle.
Springs—coil springs and telescopic shock absorbers front
and rear.
Brakes—front/rear discs/drums, servo-assisted.
Dimensions and weights—length 4330mm, width 1630mm
height 1320mm, wheelbase 2580mm, kerb weight 1130 kg.
Tyres—165 SR 13.
Capacities—engine sump 4.25 litres (7.25 Imp. pints),
cooling system 6.9 litres (12 Imp. pints), fuel tank 54
litres (11.75 Imp. gal).
  Notes—Top speed 163 km/h (101 mph).

FORD GRANADA 2800i Ghia   2793 cm³

Engine—water-cooled, V6, front mounted, bore x stroke
93 x 68.5, displacement 2792 cm³, ohv, compression
ratio 9.2:1, max. power 118 kW (160 bhp) at 5700/min,
max. torque 221 Nm (163 lb.ft) at 4300/min, Bosch K—
Jetronic fuel injection.
Transmission—rear wheels; 4-speed gearbox.
Steering—rack and pinion, servo-assisted.
Suspension—front/rear independent wishbones with anti-
roll bar/independent trailing arms.
Springs—coil springs and telescopic shock absorbers front
and rear.
Brakes—front/rear discs/drums, servo-assisted.
Dimensions and weights—length 4635mm, width 1790mm,
height 1420mm, wheelbase 2770mm, kerb weight 1380 kg.
Tyres—185 HR 14.
Capacities—engine sump 4.2 litres (7.50 Imp. pints),
cooling system 10.2 litres (17.75 Imp. pints), fuel tank
66 litres (14.50 Imp. gal).
  Top speed—193 km/h (120 mph).

FORD GRANADA 2100 DL 2112 cm^3

Engine—water-cooled, 4-cylinder, in-line, diesel, front mounted, bore x stroke 90 x 83, displacement 2112 cm^3 ohv, compression ratio 22.2:1, max. power 46 kW (63 bhp) at 4500/min, max. torque 122 Nm (90 lbf.ft) at 2000/min, Bosch fuel injection pump.
Transmission—rear wheels; 4-speed gearbox.
Steering—rack and pinion.
Suspension—front/rear independent wishbones with anti-roll bar, independent trailing arms.
Springs—coil springs and telescopic shock absorbers front and rear.
Brakes—front/rear discs/drums, servo-assisted.
Dimensions and weights—length 4635mm, width 1790 mm, height 1420mm, wheelbase 2770mm, kerb weight 1345 kg.
Tyres—175 SR 14.
Capacities—engine sump 5 litres (8.75 Imp. pints), cooling system 10 litres (17.50 Imp. pints), fuel tank 66 litres (14.50 Imp. gal).
  Top speed—137 km/h (85 mph).

FORD CAPRI 1600 S 1593 cm^3

Engine—water-cooled, 4-cylinder, in-line, front mounted, bore x stroke 87.65 x 66, displacement 1593 cm^3, ohc, compression ratio 9.2:1, max. power 65 kW (88 bhp) at 5700/min, max. torque 125 Nm (92 lbf.ft) at 4000/min, 1 Weber carburettor.

Transmission—rear wheels; 4-speed gearbox.

Steering—rack and pinion.

Suspension—front/rear McPherson struts with anti-roll bar, dead axle.

Springs—front: coil springs, rear: leaf springs, telescopic shock absorbers front and rear.

Brakes—front/rear discs/drums, servo-assisted.

Dimensions and weights—length 4370mm, width 1700mm height 1350mm, wheelbase 2560mm, kerb weight 1030kg.

Tyres—165 SR 13.

Capacities—engine sump 3.75 litres (6.50 Imp. pints), cooling system 5.8 litres (10.25 Imp. pints), fuel tank 58 litres (12.75 Imp. gal).

 Notes—Top speed 173 km/h (107 mph).

FORD MUSTANG 5.0 GHIA 4949 cm^3

Engine—water-cooled, V8, front mounted, bore x stroke
101.6 x 76.2, displacement 4949 cm^3, ohv, compression
ratio 8.4:1, max. power 135 kW (184 bhp) at 3600/min,
max. torque 240 Nm (177 lbf.ft) at 2000/min, 1 Ford
double carburettor.
Transmission—rear wheels; automatic transmission.
Steering—rack and pinion, servo-assisted.
Suspension—front/rear McPherson struts with anti-roll
bar, dead axle with Panhard rod.
Springs—coil springs and telescopic shock absorbers
front and rear.
Brakes—front/rear discs/drums, servo-assisted.
Dimensions and weights—length 4550mm, width 1750mm
height 1310mm, wheelbase 2550mm, kerb weight 1350kg.
Tyres—B78-13.
Capacities—engine sump 5 litres (8.75 Imp. pints), cooling
system 13.9 litres (24.50 Imp. pints), fuel tank 47 litres
(10.25 Imp. gal).
  Notes—Top speed 185 km/h (115 mph).

FORD FAIRMONT FUTURA 3273 cm^3

Engine—water-cooled, 6-cylinder, in-line, front mounted, bore x stroke 93.52 x 79.4, displacement 3273 cm^3, ohv, compression ratio 8.6:1, max. power 69 kW (94 bhp) at 4200/min, max. torque 152 Nm (112 lbf.ft) at 2200/min, 1 Holley single carburettor.
Transmission—rear wheels; automatic transmission.
Steering—rack and pinion, servo-assisted.
Suspension—front/rear McPherson struts with anti-roll bar, dead axle.
Springs—coil springs and telescopic shock absorbers front and rear.
Brakes—front/rear discs/drums, servo-assisted.
Dimensions and weights—length 4920mm, width 1800mm height 1360mm, wheelbase 2670mm, kerb weight 1270kg.
Tyres—DR 78-14.
Capacities—engine sump 4.7 litres (8.25 Imp. pints), cooling system 8.5 litres (15. Imp. pints), fuel tank 60 litres (13.25 Imp. gal).
   Notes—Top speed 153 km/h (95 mph).

FORD LTD LANDAU $\qquad$ 5800 cm^3

Engine—water-cooled, V8, front mounted, bore x stroke
101.6 x 88.9, displacement 5800 cm^3, ohv, compression
ratio 8.0:1, max. power 118 kW (161 bhp) at 3800/min,
max. torque 283 Nm (209 lbf.ft) at 2000/min, 1 Ford
double carburettor.
Transmission—rear wheels; automatic transmission.
Steering—recirculating ball, servo-assisted.
Suspension—front/rear independent wishbones with anti-
roll bar, dead axle with Panhard rod.
Springs—coil springs and telescopic shock absorbers front
and rear.
Brakes—front/rear discs/drums, servo-assisted.
Dimensions and weights—length 5310mm, width 1968mm
height 1400mm, wheelbase 2910mm, kerb weight 1750kg.
Tyres—GR 78-14.
Capacities—engine sump 4.3 litres (7.50 Imp. pints),
cooling system 12.6 litres (22.25 Imp. pints), fuel tank
76 litres (16.75 Imp. gal).
  Notes—Top speed 180 km/h (112 mph).

HONDA CIVIC 1200 de Luxe   1238 cm^3

Engine—water-cooled, 4-cylinder, in-line, front mounted, bore x stroke 72 x 76, displacement 1238 cm^3, ohc, compression ratio 8.1:1, max. power 44 kW (60 bhp) at 5500/min, max. torque 85 Nm (63 lbf.ft) at 3000/min, single carburettor.
Transmission—front wheels; 4-speed gearbox.
Steering—rack and pinion.
Suspension—McPherson struts with anti-roll bar, independent trailing arms.
Springs—coil springs and telescopic shock absorbers front and rear.
Brakes—front/rear dics/drums, servo-assisted.
Dimensions and weights—length 3545mm, width 1505mm height 1330mm, wheelbase 2200mm, kerb weight 695 kg.
Tyres—155 SR 13.
Capacities—engine sump 3 litres (5.25 Imp. pints), cooling system 4 litres (7 Imp. pints), fuel tank 38 litres (8.25 Imp. gal).
  Notes—Top speed 120 km/h. (74 mph)

HONDA ACCORD SEDAN   1600 cm^3

Engine—water-cooled, 4-cylinder, in-line, front mounted, bore x stroke 74 x 93, displacement 1600 cm^3, ohc, compression ratio 8.4:1, max. power 59 kW (80 bhp) at 5300/min, max. torque 125 Nm (92 lbf.ft) at 3700/min, single carburettor.
Transmission—front wheels; 5-speed gearbox.
Steering—rack and pinion.
Suspension—McPherson struts with anti-roll bar, independent trailing arms.
Springs—coil springs and telescopic shock absorbers front and rear.
Brakes—front/rear discs/drums, servo-assisted.
Dimensions and weights—length 4345mm, width 1620mm height 1360mm, wheelbase 2380mm, kerb weight 930 kg.
Tyres—155 SR13.
Capacities—engine sump 3 litres (5.25 Imp. pints), cooling system 5 litres (8.75 Imp. pints), fuel tank 50 litres (11 Imp. gal).
  Notes—Top speed 160 km/h (99 mph)

JEEP CHEROKEE   4235 cm^3

Engine—water-cooled, 6-cylinder, in-line, front mounted, bore x stroke 95.25 x 99.06, displacement 4235 cm^3, ohv, compression ratio 8:1, max. power 87 kW (118 bhp) at 3600/min, max. torque 273 Nm (201 lbf.ft) at 1800/min, 1 Carter double carburettor.
Transmission—all wheels; 3-speed gearbox.
Steering—recirculating ball.
Suspension—front/rear dead axle.
Springs—leaf springs and telescopic shock absorbers front and rear.
Brakes—front/rear discs/drums, servo-assisted.
Dimensions and weights—length 4660mm, width 1880mm height 1700mm, wheelbase 2760mm, kerb weight 1840kg.
Tyres—H78-15.
Capacities—engine sump 4.7 litres (8.25 Imp. pints), cooling system 9.9 litres (17.50 Imp. pints), fuel tank 83 litres (18.25 Imp. gal).
   Notes—Top speed 145 km/h (90 mph)

JAGUAR XJ6 4.2 SALOON   4235 cm^3

Engine—water-cooled, 6-cylinder, in-line, front mounted, bore x stroke 92 x 106, displacement 4235 cm^3, 2 x ohc compression ratio 7.8:1, max. power 125 kW (170 bhp) at 4750/min, max. torque 305 Nm (225 lbf.ft) at 3000/min, 2 SU carburettors.

Transmission—rear wheels; 5-speed gearbox.

Steering—rack and pinion, servo-assisted.

Suspension—front/rear independent wishbones with anti-roll bar, independent trailing arms.

Springs—coil springs and telescopic shock absorbers front and rear.

Brakes—front/rear discs, servo-assisted.

Dimmensions and weights—length 4945mm, width 1770 mm, height 1375mm, wheelbase 2870mm, kerb weight 1790 kg.

Tyres—205/70 VR 15.

Capacities—engine sump 8.3 litres (14.50 Imp. pints), cooling system 18.5 litres (32.50 Imp. pints), fuel tank 91 litres (20 Imp. gal).

  Notes—USA version with fuel injection L-Jetronic (129 kW).

  Notes—Top speed 195 km/h (121 mph)

JAGUAR XJS

5343cm^3

Engine—water-cooled, V12, front mounted, bore x stroke
90 x 70, displacement 5343 cm^3, 2 ohc, compression
ratio 9:1, max. power 213 kW (290 bhp) at 5500/min,
max. torque 399 Nm (294 lbf.ft) at 3500/min, Bosch/
Lucas fuel-injection.
Transmission—rear wheels; automatic transmission GM.
Steering—rack and pinion, servo-assisted.
Suspension—front/rear independent wishbones with anti-
roll bar, independent trailing arms.
Springs—coil springs and telescopic shock absorbers front
and rear.
Brakes—front/rear, discs, servo-assisted.
Dimensions and weights—length 4838mm, width 1793mm
height 1244mm, wheelbase 2591mm, kerb weight 1721kg.
Tyres—205/70 VR 15.
Capacities—engine sump 11 litres (19.25 Imp. pints),
cooling system 21 litres (37 Imp. pints), fuel tank 91
litres (20 Imp. gal).
  Notes—Top speed 241 km/h (150 mph)

LADA 1300 $1294\ cm^3$

Engine—water-cooled, 4-cylinder, in-line, front mounted, bore x stroke 79 x 66, displacement 1294 cm^3, ohc, compression ratio 8.5:1, max. power 51 kW (69 bhp) at 5600/min, max. torque 96 Nm (71 lbf.ft) at 3400/min, 1 Weber carburettor.

Transmission—rear wheels; 4-speed gearbox.

Steering—worm and roller.

Suspension—front/rear independent wishbones with anti-roll bar, trailing arms, dead axle.

Springs—coil springs and telescopic shock absorbers front and rear.

Brakes—front/rear discs/drums, servo-assisted.

Dimensions and weights—length 4043mm, width 1611mm height 1440mm, wheelbase 2424mm, kerb weight 955 kg.

Tyres—165 SR13.

Capacities—engine sump 3.8 litres (6.75 Imp. pints), cooling system 9.6 litres (17 Imp. pints), fuel tank 39 litres (8.50 Imp. gal.)

   Notes—Top speed 145 km/h (90 mph)

LADA 1600GL

1568cm^3

Engine—water-cooled, 4-cylinder, in-line, front mounted, bore x stroke 79 x 80, displacement 1568 cm^3, ohc, compression ratio 8.8:1, max. power 57 kW (78 bhp) at 5200/min, max. torque 122 Nm (90 lbf.ft) at 3400/min, 1 Weber carburettor.
Transmission—rear wheels; 4-speed gearbox.
Steering—worm and roller.
Suspension—front/rear independent wishbones with anti-roll bar, trailing arms, dead axle.
Springs—coil springs and telescopic shock absorbers front and rear.
Brakes—front/rear discs/drums, servo-assisted.
Dimensions and weights—length 4090mm, width 1611mm height 1440mm, wheelbase 2424mm, kerb weight 1050kg.
Tyres—165 SR13.
Capacities—engine sump 3.8 litres (6.75 Imp. pints), cooling system 9.6 litres (17 Imp. pints), fuel tank 39 litres (8.50 Imp. gal).
   Notes—Top speed 154 km/h (96 mph)

LADA NIVA 2121   1570 cm^3

Engine—water-cooled, 4-cylinder, in-line, front mounted, bore x stroke 79 x 80, displacement 1570 cm^3, ohc, compression ratio 8.5:1, max. power 57 kW (78 bhp) at 5400/min, max. torque 120 Nm (89 lbf.ft) at 3000/min, 1 Weber carburettor.
Transmission—all wheels; 4-speed gearbox.
Steering—worm and roller.
Suspension—front/rear independent wishbones with anti-roll bar trailing, dead axle.
Springs—coil springs and telescopic shock absorbers front and rear.
Brakes—front/rear discs/drums, servo-assisted.
Dimensions and weights—length 3735mm, width 1680mm height 1645mm, wheelbase 2200mm, kerb weight 1150 kg.
Tyres—6.95-16
Capacities—engine sump 3.75 litres (6.50 Imp. pints), cooling system 10.6 litres (18.75 Imp. pints), fuel tank 45 litres (10 Imp. gal).
  Notes—Top speed 132 km/h (82 mph)

LAMBORGHINI JARAMA GTS 3929 cm³

Engine—water-cooled, V12, front mounted, bore x stroke
82 x 62, displacement 3929 cm³, 2 x dohc, compression
ratio 10.7:1, max. power 268 kW (364 bhp) at 7500/min,
max. torque 407 Nm (300 lbf.ft) at 5500/min, 6 Weber
double carburettors.
Transmission—rear wheels; 5-speed gearbox.
Steering—worm and roller.
Suspension—struts independent wishbones with anti-
roll bar.
Springs—coil springs and telescopic shock absorbers front
and rear.
Brakes—front/rear discs, servo-assisted.
Dimensions and weights—length 4485mm, width 1820mm
height 1190mm, wheelbase 2380mm, kerb weight 1540kg.
Tyres—215/70 VR15.
Capacities—engine sump 14.3 litres (25.25 Imp. pints),
cooling system 14 litres (24.75 Imp. pints), fuel tank
100 litres (22 Imp. gal).
  Notes—Top speed 260 km/h (161 mph)

LANCIA BETA 1600   1585cm^3

Engine—water-cooled, 4-cylinder, in-line, front mounted, bore x stroke 84 x 71.5, displacement 1585 cm^3, dohc, compression ratio 9.4:1, max. power 74 kW (101 bhp) at 5800/min, max. torque 134 Nm (99 lbf.ft) at 3000/min, 1 Weber carburettor.

Transmission—front wheels; 5-speed gearbox.

Steering—rack and pinion.

Suspension—front/rear McPherson struts with anti-roll bar., independent trailing arms.

Springs—coil springs and telescopic shock absorbers front and rear.

Brakes—front/rear discs/discs, servo-assisted.

Dimensions and weights—length 4295mm, width 1706 mm, height 1400mm, wheelbase 2540mm, kerb weight 1100 kg.

Tyres—175/70 SR 14

Capacities—engine sump 4.2 litres (7.25 Imp. pints), cooling system 7.6 litres (13.25 Imp. pints), fuel tank 49 litres (10.75 Imp. gal).

   Notes—For North America (SAE) 1756 cm^3, 84 x 79.2 8.0:1, 64 kW, 123 Nm.

   Notes—Top speed 178 km/h (111 mph)

LANCIA HPE 2000

1995 cm^3

Engine—water-cooled, 4-cylinder, in-line, front mounted, bore x stroke 84 x 90, displacement 1995 cm^3, dohc, compression ratio 8.9:1, max. power 88 kW (120 bhp) at 5500/min, max. torque 174 Nm (128 lbf.ft) at 2800/min, 1 Weber carburettor.

Transmission—front wheels; 5-speed gearbox.

Steering—rack and pinion.

Suspension—front/rear McPherson struts with anti-roll bar, independent trailing arms.

Springs—coil springs and telescopic shock absorbers front and rear.

Brakes—front/rear—discs, servo-assisted.

Dimensions and weights—length 4285mm, width 1650mm height 1310mm, wheelbase 2540mm, kerb weight 1060kg.

Tyres—175/70 SR14.

Capacities—engine sump 4.5 litres (8 Imp. pints), cooling system 7.6 litres (13.25 Imp. pints), fuel tank 52 litres (11.50 Imp. gal).

    Notes—Top speed 188 km/h (117 mph)

LANCIA GAMMA BERLINA 2484 cm^3

Engine—water-cooled, 4-cylinder, flat engine, front mounted, bore x stroke 102 x 76, displacement 2484 cm^3 dohc, compression ratio 9:1, max. power 103 kW (140 bhp) at 5400/min, max. torque 208 Nm (154 lbf.ft) at 3000/min, 1 Weber double carburettor.
Transmission—front wheels; 5-speed gearbox.
Steering—rack and pinion, servo-assisted.
Suspension—front/rear McPherson struts with anti-roll bar, independent trailing arms.
Springs—coil springs and telescopic shock absorbers front and rear.
Brakes—front/rear discs/discs, servo-assisted.
Dimensions and weights—length 4580mm, width 1730mm height 1410mm, wheelbase 2670mm, kerb weight 1320kg.
Tyres—185/70 HR14.
Capacities—engine sump 6.1 litres (10.75 Imp. pints), cooling system 9 litres (15.50 Imp. pints), fuel tank 63 litres (14 Imp. gal).
  Notes—Top speed 195 km/h (121 mph)

LANCIA BETA MONTE CARLO   1995 cm^3

Engine—water-cooled, 4-cylinder, in-line, centre mounted, bore x stroke 84 x 90, displacement 1995 cm^3, dohc, compression ratio 9.35:1, max. power 89 kW (121 bhp) at 6000/min, max. torque 171 Nm (126 lbf.ft) at 3400/min, 1 Weber double carburettor.
Transmission—rear wheels; 5-speed gearbox.
Steering—rack and pinion.
Suspension—front/rear McPherson struts with anti-roll bar, independent trailing arms.
Springs—coil springs and telescopic shock absorbers front and rear.
Brakes—front/rear discs/discs, servo-assisted.
Dimensions and weights—length 3813mm, width 1696mm height 1190mm, wheelbase 2300mm, kerb weight 1040kg.
Tyres—185/70 HR 13.
Capacities—engine sump 6.2 litres (11 Imp. pints), cooling system 14 litres (24.75 Imp. pints), fuel tank 59 litres (13 Imp. gal).
  Notes—Top speed 190 km/h (118 mph). Engine for North America: see HPE.

LOTUS ECLAT 521   1973 cm^3

Engine—water-cooled, 4-cylinder, in-line, front mounted, bore x stroke 95 x 63, displacement 1973 cm^3, dohc, compression ratio 9.5:1, max. power 119 kW (162 bhp) at 6200/min, max. torque 190 Nm (140 lbf.ft) at 4900/min, 2 Dell'Orto double carburettors.
Transmission—rear wheels; 5-speed gearbox.
Steering—rack and pinion.
Suspension—front/rear independent wishbones with anti-roll bar, independent trailing arms.
Springs—coil springs and telescopic shock absorbers front and rear.
Brakes—front/rear discs/drums, servo-assisted.
Dimensions and weights—length 4460mm, width 1820mm height 1210mm, wheelbase 2480mm, kerb weight 980 kg.
Tyres—205/60 HR 14.
Capacities—engine sump 6 litres (10.50 Imp. pints), cooling system 8.5 litres (15 Imp. pints), fuel tank 68 litres (15 Imp. gal).

  Notes—Top speed 208 km/h (129 mph)

LOTUS ESPRIT S2   1973 cm^3

Engine—water-cooled, 4-cylinder, in-line, centre mounted, bore x stroke 95 x 63, displacement 1973 cm^3, dohc, compression ratio 9.5:1, max. power 119 kW (162 bhp) at 6200/min, max. torque 190 Nm (140 lbf.ft) at 4900/min. 2 Dell'Orto double carburettorrs.
Transmission—rear wheels; 5-speed gearbox.
Steering—rack and pinion.
Suspension—front/rear independent wishbones with anti-roll bar, independent trailing arms.
Springs—coil springs and telescopic shock absorbers front and rear.
Brakes—front/rear discs, servo-assisted.
Dimensions and weights—length 4190mm, width 1860mm height 1110mm, wheelbase 2440mm, kerb weight 900 kg.
Tyres—front: 195/70 HR14; rear: 205/70 HR 14.
Capacities—engine sump 6 litres (10.50 Imp. pints), cooling system 8.5 litres (15 Imp. pints), fuel tank 68 litres (15 Imp. gal).
   Notes—Top speed 220 km/h (136 mph)

MASERATI MERAK SS $2965\ cm^3$

Engine—water-cooled, V6, in-line, rear mounted, bore x stroke 91.6 x 75, displacement $2965\ cm^3$, 2 x dohc, compression ratio 9:1, max. power 162 kW (220 bhp) at 6500/min, max. torque 270 Nm (199 lbf.ft) at 4500/min, 3 Weber double carburettors.
Transmission—rear wheels; 5-speed gearbox.
Steering—rack and pinion.
Suspension—front/rear McPherson with anti-roll bar independent railing arms.
Springs—coil springs and telescopic shock absorbers front and rear.
Brakes—front/rear discs, servo-assisted.
Dimensions and weights—length 4335mm, width 1770mm height 1135mm, wheelbase 2600mm, kerb weight 1350kg.
Tyres—front: 195/70 VR 15; rear 215/70 VR 15.
Capacities—engine sump 7 litres (12.25 Imp. pints), cooling system 14 litres (24.75 Imp. pints), fuel tank 85 litres(18.75 Imp. gal).
   Notes—Top speed 250 km/h (155 mph)

MATRA SIMCA BAGHEERA S 1442 cm^3

Engine—water-cooled, 4-cylinder, in-line, front mounted, bore x stroke 76.7 x 78, displacement 1442 cm^3, ohv, compression ratio 9.5:1, max. power 66 kW (90 bhp) at 5800/min, max. torque 120 Nm (89 lbf.ft) at 3200/min, 2 Weber carburettors.
Transmission—rear wheels; 4-speed gearbox.
Steering—rack and pinion.
Suspension—front/rear independent wishbones with anti-roll bar, independent trailing arms.
Springs—torsions bars and telescopic shock absorbers front and rear.
Brakes—front/rear discs, servo-assisted.
Dimensions and weights—length 4010mm, width 1734 mm, height 1220mm, wheelbase 2370mm, kerb weight 1015 kg.
Tyres—front: 155 HR 13, rear: 185 HR 13.
Capacities—engine sump 3.3 litres (5.75 Imp. pints), cooling system 10.5 litres (18.50 Imp. pints), fuel tank 56 litres (12.25 Imp. gal.)
   Notes—Top speed 185 km/h (115 mph)

MATRA SIMCA RANCHO   1442 cm³

Engine—water-cooled, 4-cylinder, in-line, front mounted, bore x stroke 76.8 x 78, displacement 1442 cm³, ohv, compression ratio 9.5:1, max. power 59 kW (80 bhp) at 5600/min, max. torque 118 Nm (87 lbf.ft) at 3000/min, 1 Weber single carburettor.
Transmission—front wheels; 4-speed gearbox.
Steering—rack and pinion.
Suspension—front/rear independent wishbones with anti-roll bar, independent trailing arms.
Springs—front torsion bars, telescopic shock absorbers front and rear.
Brakes—front/rear discs/drums, servo-assisted.
Dimensions and weights—length 4315mm, width 1665 mm, height 1735mm, wheelbase 2520mm, kerb weight 1129 kg.
Tyres—185/70 HR 14.
Capacities—engine sump 3.3 litres (5.75 Imp. pints), cooling system 6 litres (10.50 Imp. pints), fuel tank 60 litres (13.25 Imp. gal).
   Notes—Top speed 145 km/h (90 mph)

MAZDA MONTROSE (626)   1586 cm^3

Engine—water-cooled, 4-cylinder, in-line, front mounted, bore x stroke 78 x 83, displacement 1586 cm^3, 1 x ohc, compression ratio 8.6:1, max. power 55 kW (75 bhp) at 5000/min, max. torque 119 Nm (81 lbf.ft) at 3800/min, 1 twin choke two stage carburettor.
Transmission—rear wheels; 4-speed manual gearbox.
Steering—recirculating ball, variable ratio.
Suspension—front: coil springs, rear: coil springs and gas filled telescopic shock absorbers front and rear.
Panhard rod and upper torque rods.
Brakes—front/rear discs/drums, servo-assisted, dual circuit.
Dimensions and weights—length 4305mm, width 1660mm, height 1370mm, wheelbase 2510mm, kerb weight 1065kg.
Tyres—165SR-13 (2000 cm^3 models: 185-70)
Capacities—engine sump 4.1 litres (7.25 Imp. pints), cooling system 7.5 litres (13.25 Imp. pints), fuel tank 55 litres (12 Imp. gal).
   Notes—Also available with a 2000 cm^3 engine option and a 2000 cm^3 Coupe version. Automatic Transmission available as optional extra with 2000 cm^3 Saloon version only. 5-speed manual as standard on 2000 cm^3 models. Top speed: 160 km/h (99 mph). Also known as "Capella" in its own domestic market.

MAZDA 323 SP 1.4   1415 cm^3

Engine—water-cooled, 4-cylinder, in-line, front mounted,
bore x stroke 77 x 76, displacement 1415 cm^3, ohc,
compression ratio 9:1, max. power 51 kW (69 bhp) at
5700/min, max. torque 112 Nm (83 lbf.ft) at 3200/min,
1 Hitachi carburettor.
Transmission—rear wheels; 4-speed gearbox.
Steering—recirculating ball.
Suspension—front/rear McPherson struts with anti-roll
bar, dead axle with Panhard rod.
Springs—coil springs and telescopic shock absorbers
front and rear.
Brakes—front/rear discs/drums, servo-assisted.
Dimensions and weights—length 3910mm, width 1605mm
height 1375mm, wheelbase 2315mm, kerb weight 845 kg.
Tyres—175/70 SR 13.
Capacities—engine sump 3 litres (5.25 Imp. pints), cooling
system 5.5 litres (9.50 Imp. pints), fuel tank 45 litres
(10 Imp. gal).
  Notes—Top speed 146 km/h (91 mph).

MAZDA 818 S

1272 cm^3

Engine—water-cooled, 4-cylinder, in-line, front mounted, bore x stroke 73 x 76, displacement 1272 cm^3, ohc, compression ratio 9.2:1, max. power 48 kW (65 bhp) at 6000/min, max. torque 92 Nm (68 lbf.ft) at 3500/min, 1 Nikki single carburettor.
Transmission—rear wheels; 4-speed gearbox.
Steering—recirculating ball, .
Suspension—front/rear McPherson struts with anti-roll bar, dead axle.
Springs—front: coil springs, rear: leaf springs, telescopic shock absorbers front and rear.
Brakes—front/rear discs/drums, servo-assisted.
Dimensions and weights—length 4075mm, width 1595mm height 1380mm, wheelbase 2310mm, kerb weight 850 kg.
Tyres—155 SR 13.
Capacities—engine sump 3.3 litres (6 Imp. pints), cooling system 5.6 litres (10 Imp. pints), fuel tank 45 litres (10 Imp. gal).
  Notes—Top speed 150 km/h (93 mph).

MAZDA 616 LN   1586 cm^3

Engine—water-cooled, 4-cylinder, in-line, front mounted,
bore x stroke 78 x 83, displacement 1586 cm^3, ohc,
compression ratio 8.6:1, max. power 55 kW (75 bhp) at
5000/min, max. torque 116 Nm (86 lbf.ft) at 3500/min,
1 Nikki carburettor.
Transmission—rear wheels; 4-speed gearbox.
Steering—recirculating ball.
Suspension—front/rear McPherson struts with anti-roll
bar, dead axle with Panhard rod.
Springs—coil springs and telescopic shock absorbers front
and rear.
Brakes—front/rear discs/drums, servo-assisted.
Dimensions and weights—length 4260mm, width 1580mm
height 1435mm, wheelbase 2470mm, kerb weight 970 kg.
Tyres—165 SR 13.
Capacities—engine sump 3.6 litres (6.25 Imp. pints),
cooling system 7 litres (12.25 Imp. pints), fuel tank
50 litres (11 Imp. gal).
   Notes—Top speed 165 km/h (102 mph).

MAZDA 929 S   1769 cm^3

Engine—water-cooled, 4-cylinder, in-line, front mounted, bore x stroke 80 x 88, displacement 1769 cm^3, ohc, compression ratio 8.6:1, max. power 61 kW (83 bhp) at 5000/min, max. torque 138 Nm (102 lbf.ft) at 2900/min, 1 Hitachi carburettor.
Transmission—rear wheels; 4-speed gearbox.
Steering—recirculating ball, servo-assisted.
Suspension—front/rear McPherson struts with anti-roll bar, dead axle.
Springs—front: coil springs, rear: leaf springs, telescopic shock absorbers front and rear.
Brakes—front/rear discs/drums, servo-assisted.
Dimensions and weights—length 4400mm, width 1660mm height 1410mm, wheelbase 2510mm, kerb weight 1050kg.
Tyres—175 SR 13.
Capacities—engine sump 3.6 litres (6.25 Imp. pints), cooling system 7.5 litres (13.25 Imp. pints), fuel tank 65 litres (14.25 Imp. gal).
   Notes—Top speed 165 km/h (102 mph).

MAZDA 121 LANDAU $1769\ cm^3$

Engine—water-cooled, 4-cylinder, in-line, front mounted, bore x stroke 80 x 88, displacement 1769 cm^3, ohc, compression ratio 8.6:1, max. power 61 kW (83 bhp) at 5000/min, max. torque 134 Nm (99 lbf.ft) at 2500/min, 1 Nikki carburettor.
Transmission—rear wheels; 5-speed gearbox.
Steering—recirculating ball.
Suspension—front/rear McPherson struts with anti-roll bar, dead axle with Panhard rod.
Springs—coil springs and telescopic shock absorbers front and rear.
Brakes—front/rear discs, servo-assisted.
Dimensions and weights—length 4475mm, width 1685mm height 1325mm, wheelbase 2510mm, kerb weight 1140kg.
Tyres—185/70 SR 14.
Capacities—engine sump 3.6 litres (6.25 Imp. pints), cooling system 7.5 litres (13.25 Imp. pints), fuel tank 65 litres (14.25 Imp. gal).
  Notes—Top speed 170 km/h (106 mph).

MAZDA LEGATO AUTOMATIC 1970 cm^3

Engine—water-cooled, 4-cylinder, in-line, front mounted, bore x stroke 80 x 98, displacement 1970 cm^3, 1 ohc, compression ratio 8.6:1, max. power 66 kW (90 bhp) at 4800/min, max. torque 160 Nm (118 lbf.ft) at 2500/min 1 Nikki/Stromberg carburettor.
Transmission—rear wheels; automatic Rematic transmission.
Steering—recirculating ball.
Suspension—front/rear McPherson struts with anti-roll bar, dead axle with Panhard rod.
Springs—coil springs and telescopic shock absorbers front and rear.
Brakes—front/rear discs/drums, servo-assisted.
Dimensions and weights—length 4645mm, width 1710mm height 1415mm, wheelbase 2610mm, kerb weight 1160kg.
Tyres—175 SR 14.
Capacities—engine sump 4.4 litres (7.75 Imp. pints), cooling system 8 litres (14 Imp. pints), fuel tank 65 litres (14.25 Imp. gal.).
   Notes—Top speed 155 km/h (96 mph)

MAZDA RX-7

$2 \times 573 \text{cm}^3$

Engine—water-cooled, Wankel engine with two co-axial rotors; front mounted, displacement $2 \times 573 \text{ cm}^3$, compression ratio 9.4:1, max. power 74 kW (101 bhp) at 6000/min, max. torque 156 Nm (115 lbf.ft) at 4000/min, 1 Nikki four-barrel carburettor.
Transmission—rear wheels; 4-speed gearbox.
Steering—recirculating ball.
Suspension—front/rear McPherson struts with anti-roll bar dead axle.
Springs—coil springs and telescopic shock absorbers front and rear.
Brakes—front/rear discs/drums, servo-assisted.
Dimensions and weights—length 4265mm, width 1650mm height 1260mm, wheelbase 2420mm, kerb weight 1009kg.
Tyres—not known.
Capacities—engine sump 5.2 litres (9 Imp. pints), cooling system 8.8 litres (15.50 Imp. pints), fuel tank 55 litres (12 Imp. gal).
  Notes—Top speed 190 km/h (118 mph)

MERCEDES-BENZ 200D

1988 cm^3

Engine—water-cooled, 4-cylinder, diesel, front mounted, bore x stroke 87 x 83.6, displacement 1988 cm^3, ohc, compression ratio 21:1, max. power 40 kW (54 bhp) at 4200/min, max. torque 113 Nm (83 lbf.ft) at 2400/min Bosch fuel injection pump.
Transmission—rear wheels; 4-speed gearbox.
Steering—recirculating ball.
Suspension—front/rear independent wishbones with anti-roll bar, independent trailing arms.
Springs—coil springs and telescopic shock absorbers front and rear.
Brakes—front/rear discs, servo-assisted.
Dimensions and weights—length 4725mm, width 1786mm height 1438mm, wheelbase 2795mm, kerb weight 1375mm
Tyres—175 SR 14.
Capacities—engine sump 6.5 litres (11.50 Imp. pints), cooling system 10.2 litres (17.75 Imp. pints), fuel tank 65 litres (14.25 Imp. gal).
  Notes—Top speed 130 km/h. (81 mph)

MERCEDES-BENZ 230 T   2307 cm^3

Engine—water-cooled, 4-cylinder, in-line, front mounted,
bore x stroke 93.75 x 83.6, displacement 2307 cm^3, ohc,
compression ratio 9:1, max. power 80 kW (109 bhp) at
4800/min, max. torque 186 Nm (137 lbf.ft) at 3000/min
1 Stromberg single carburettor.
Transmission—rear wheels; automatic transmission MB.
Steering—recirculating ball.
Suspension—front/rear independent wishbones with anti-
roll bar, independent trailing arms.
Springs—coil springs and telescopic shock absorbers front
and rear, rear levelling control.
Brakes—front/rear discs, servo-assisted.
Dimensions and weights—length 4730mm, width 1790mm
height 1470mm, wheelbase 2800mm, kerb weight 1450kg.
Tyres—195/70 SR 14.
Capacities—engine sump 5 litres (8.75 Imp. pints), cooling
system 10 litres (17.50 Imp. pints), fuel tank 70 litres
(15.50 Imp. gal)'.
  Notes—Top speed 165 km/h. (102 mph)
USA version: 64 kW @ 4800/min, 157 Nm @ 3000/min.

MERCEDES-BENZ 300D   3005 cm³

Engine—water-cooled, 5-cylinder, in-line, diesel, front mounted, bore x stroke 91 x 92.4, displacement 3005 cm³ ohc, compression ratio 21:1, max. power 59 kW (80 bhp) at 4000/min, max. torque 172 Nm (127 lbf.ft) at 2400/min,

Transmission—rear wheels; 4-speed gearbox.

Steering—recirculating ball, servo assisted.

Suspension—front/rear independent wishbones with anti-roll bar, independent trailing arms.

Springs—coil springs and telescopic shock absorbers front and rear.

Brakes—front/rear discs, servo-assisted.

Dimensions and weights—length 4725mm, width 1786mm height 1438mm, wheelbase 2795mm, kerb weight 1445kg.

Tyres—175 SR 14.

Capacities—engine sump 6.5 litres (11.50 Imp. pints), cooling system 11 litres (19.25 Imp. pints), fuel tank 65 litres (14.25 Imp. gal).

   Notes—Top speed 148 km/h. (92 mph)

MERCEDES-BENZ 280CE 2746 cm³

Engine—water-cooled, 6-cylinder, in-line, front mounted, bore x stroke 86 x 78.8, displacement 2746 cm³, dohc, compression ratio 8.7:1, max. power 130 kW (177 bhp) at 6000/min, max. torque 234 Nm (173 lbf.ft) at 4500/min, Bosch K-Jetronic fuel-injection.
Transmission—rear wheels; 4-speed gearbox.
Steering—recirculating ball, servo-assisted.
Suspension—front/rear independent wishbones with anti-roll bar, independent trailing arms.
Springs—coil springs and telescopic shock absorbers front and rear.
Brakes—front/rear discs, servo-assisted.
Dimensions and weights—length 4640mm, width 1786mm height 1395mm, wheelbase 2710mm, kerb weight 1450kg.
Tyres—195/70 HR 14.
Capacities—engine sump 6 litres (10.50 Imp. pints), cooling system 10 litres (17.50 Imp. pints), fuel tank 80 litres (17.50 Imp. gal).
  Notes—Top speed 200 km/h (124 mph)

MERCEDES-BENZ 350 SE   3499 cm^3

Engine—water-cooled, V8, front mounted, bore x stroke
92 x 65.8, displacement 3499 cm^3, 2 x ohc, compression
ratio 9:1, max. power 151 kW (205 bhp) at 5750/min,
max. torque 285 Nm (210 lbf.ft) at 4000/min, Bosch K-
Jetronic fuel injection.
Transmission—rear wheels; 4-speed gearbox.
Steering—recirculating ball, servo-assisted.
Suspension—front/rear independent wishbones with anti-
roll bar, independent trailing arms.
Springs—coil springs and telescopic shock absorbers front
and rear.
Brakes—front/rear discs, servo-assisted.
Dimensions and weights—length 4960mm, width 1870mm,
height 1425mm, wheelbase 2865mm, kerb weight 1675kg.
Tyres—205/70 HR 14.
Capacities—engine sump 8 litres (14 Imp. pints), cooling
system 13.5 litres (23.75 Imp. pints), fuel tank 96 litres
(21. Imp. gal).
   Notes—Top speed 205 km/h (127 mph)

MERCEDES-BENZ 450 SEL 6.9   6834 cm^3

Engine—water-cooled, V8-cylinder, front mounted, bore x stroke 107 x 95, displacement 6834 cm^3, 2 x ohc, compression ratio 8.8:1, max. power 210 kW (285 bhp) at 4250/min, max. torque 550 Nm (406 lbf.ft) at 3000/min, Bosch K-Jetronic fuel injection.
Transmission—rear wheels; automatic transmission.
Steering—recirculating ball, servo-assisted.
Suspension—front/rear independent wishbones with anti-roll bar, independent trailing arms.
Springs—hydro-pneumatic system and telescopic shock absorbers front and rear (automatic levelling control front and rear).
Brakes—front/rear discs, servo-assisted.
Dimensions and weights—length 5060mm, width 1870mm height 1440mm, wheelbase 2960mm, kerb weight 1935kg.
Tyres—215/70 VR 14.
Capacities—engine sump 11 litres (19.25 Imp. pints), cooling system 16 litres (28.25 Imp. pints), fuel tank 96 litres (21 Imp. gal).
  Notes—Top speed 225 km/h (140 mph).

MERCEDES 450 SLC 5.0   5025 cm^3

Engine—water-cooled, V8, front mounted, bore x stroke 97 x 85, displacement 5025 cm^3, 2 x ohc, compression ratio 8.8:1, max. power 177 Kw (241 bhp) at 5000/min max. torque 404 Nm (298 lbf.ft) at 3200/min, Bosch K-Jetronic fuel injection.
Transmission—rear wheels; automatic transmission/MB-Automat.
Steering—recirculating ball, servo-assisted.
Suspension—front/rear independent wishbones with anti-roll bar/independent longitudinal trailing arms.
Springs—coil springs, auxiliary rubber springs and telescopic shock absorbers front and rear.
Brakes—front/rear discs, servo-assisted.
Dimensions and weights—length 4750mm, width 1790 mm, height 1330mm, wheelbase 2815mm, kerb weight 1515kg.
Tyres—205/70 VR 14.
Capacities—engine sump 9 litres (16. Imp. pints), cooling system 12.5 litres (22 Imp. pints), fuel tank 90 litres (20 Imp. gal.)
  Notes—Top speed 230 km/h (143 mph)

MERCURY ZEPHYR   3273 cm^3

Engine—water-cooled, 6-cylinder, in-line, front mounted,
bore x stroke 93.52 x 79.4, displacement 3273 cm^3, ohv
compression ratio 8.6:1, max. power 69 kW (94 bhp) at
4200/min, max. torque 152 Nm (112 lbf.ft) at 2200/min,
1 Holley single carburettor.
Transmission—rear wheels; automatic transmission.
Steering—rack and pinion, servo-assisted.
Suspension—front/rear McPherson struts with anti-roll
bar, dead axle.
Springs—coil springs and telescopic shock absorbers front
and rear.
Brakes—front/rear discs/drums, servo-assisted.
Dimensions and weights—length 4990mm, width 1800mm
height 1420mm, wheelbase 2670mm, kerb weight 1270kg.
Tyres—DR 78-14.
Capacities—engine sump 4.7 litres (8.25 Imp. pints),
cooling system 8.5 litres (15. Imp. pints), fuel tank 60
litres (13.25 Imp. gal).
  Notes—Top speed 158 km/h (98 mph).

MINI 1100 SPECIAL

1098 cm³

Engine—water-cooled, 4-cylinder, in-line, front mounted, bore x stroke 64.58 x 83.72, displacement 1098 cm³, ohv, compression ratio 8.5:1, max. power 33 kW (45 bhp) at 5250/min, max. torque 76 Nm (56 lbf.ft) at 2700/min, 1 SU carburettor.

Transmission—front wheels; 4-speed gearbox.

Steering—rack and pinion.

Suspension—front/rear independent wishbones, independent trailing arms.

Springs—rubber cones and telescopic shock absorbers front and rear.

Brakes—front/rear drums/drums.

Dimensions and weights—length 3071mm, width 1410mm height 1346mm, wheelbase 2030mm, kerb weight 620 kg.

Tyres—145 SR 10 ZX.

Capacities—engine sump 4.8 litres (8.50 Imp. pints), cooling system 3.6 litres (6.25 Imp. pints), fuel tank 25 litres (5.50 Imp. gal).

   Notes—Top speed 144 km/h (89 mph).

MITSUBISHI (COLT)
LANCER 1400 GL AUTOMATIC   1439 cm³

Engine—water-cooled, 4-cylinder, in-line, front mounted, bore x stroke 73 x 86, displacement 1439 cm³, ohc, compression ratio 9:1, max. power 50 kW (68 bhp) at 5000/min, max. torque 104 Nm (77 lbf.ft) at 4000/min, 1 Solex single carburettor.

Transmission—rear wheels, Chrysler automatic transmission.

Steering—recirculating ball.

Suspension—front/rear McPherson struts, dead axle.

Springs—front: coil springs, rear: leaf springs, telescopic shock absobers front and rear.

Brakes—front/rear discs/drums, servo-assisted.

Dimensions and weights—length 3995mm, width 1535mm height 1360mm, wheelbase 2340mm, kerb weight 995 kg.

Tyres—155SR 13.

Capacities—engine sump 3.5 litres (6.25 Imp. pints), cooling system 6 litres (10.50 Imp. pints), fuel tank 50 litres (11 Imp. gal).

  Notes—Top speed 165 km/h (102 mph).

MITSUBISHI (COLT)
GALANT SIGMA 1600 GL   1597 cm³

Engine—water-cooled, 4-cylinder, in-line, front mounted,
bore x stroke 76.9 x 86, displacement 1597 cm³, ohc,
compression ratio 8.5:1, max. power 55 kW (75 bhp) at
5000/min, max. torque 115 Nm (85 lbf.ft) at 4000/min,
1 Solex carburettor.
Transmission—rear wheels; 4-speed gearbox.
Steering—recirculating ball.
Suspension—front/rear McPherson struts with anti-roll
bar, dead axle.
Springs—coil springs and telescopic shock absorbers front
and rear.
Brakes—front/rear discs/drums, servo-assisted.
Dimensions and weights—length 4300mm, width 1655mm
height 1355mm, wheelbase 2515mm, kerb weight 1005kg.
Tyres—165 SR 13.
Capacities—engine sump 4 litres (7 Imp. pints), cooling
system 7.2 litres (12.75 Imp. pints), fuel tank 60 litres
(13.25 Imp. gal).
  Notes—Top speed 155 km/h (96 mph).

MITSUBISHI (COLT) CELESTE 2000 GT

1995 cm³

Engine—water-cooled, 4-cylinder, in-line, front mounted, bore x stroke 84 x 90, displacement 1995 cm³, ohc, compression ratio 8.5:1, max. power 62 kW (84 bhp) at 5000/min, max. torque 132 Nm (101 lbf.ft) at 3500/min, 1 Solex carburettor.
Transmission—rear wheels; 5-speed gearbox.
Steering—recirculating ball.
Suspension—front/rear McPherson struts with anti-roll bar, dead axle.
Springs—front: coil springs, rear: leaf springs, telescopic shock absorbers front and rear.
Brakes—front/rear discs/drums, servo-assisted.
Dimensions and weights—length 4115, (USA 4250)mm, height 1330mm, wheelbase 2340mm, width 1610mm, kerb weight 990 kg.
Tyres—175/70 HR 13.
Capacities—engine sump 3.8 litres (6.75 Imp. pints), cooling system 7.7 litres (13.50 Imp. pints), fuel tank 45 litres (10 Imp. gal).
  Notes—Top speed 170 km/h (106 mph).

MITSUBISHI (COLT)
GALANT SAPPORO SL
1995 cm³

Engine—water-cooled, 4-cylinder, in-line, front mounted, bore x stroke 84 x 90, displacement 1995 cm³, ohc, compression ratio 8.5:1, max. power 66 kW (90 bhp) at 5250/min, max. torque 139 Nm (103 lbf.ft) at 3000/min, 1 Solex carburettor.

Transmission—rear wheels, Chrysler automatic transmission.

Steering—recirculating ball.

Suspension—front/rear McPherson struts with anti-roll bar, dead axle.

Springs—coil springs and telescopic shock absorbers front and rear.

Brakes—front/rear discs, servo-assisted.

Dimensions and weights—length 4430mm, width 1675mm height 1330mm, wheelbase 2515mm, kerb weight 1140kg.

Tyres—195/70 HR 14.

Capacities—engine sump 3.8 litres (6.75 Imp. pints), cooling system 7.5 litres (13.25 Imp. pints), fuel tank 60 litres (13.25 Imp. gal).

Notes—Top speed 160 km/h (99 mph).

MORGAN PLUS 8 3528 cm^3

Engine—water-cooled, V8, front mounted, bore x stroke
88.9 x 71, displacement 3528 cm^3, 5 ohv, compression
ratio 9.35:1, max. power 115 kW (156 bhp) at 5250/min,
max. torque 267 Nm (197 lbf.ft) at 2500/min, 2 SU
carburettors.
Transmission—rear wheels; 5-speed gearbox.
Steering—worm and roller.
Suspension—front/rear independent wishbones, dead axle.
Springs—front coil springs and telescopic shock absorbers;
rear transversal leaf springs and lever shock absorbers.
Brakes—front/rear discs/drums, servo-assisted.
Dimensions and weights—length 3730mm, width 1580mm
height 1320mm, wheelbase 2490mm, kerb weight 830 kg.
Tyres—195 VR 14.
Capacities—engine sump 5.5 litres (9.75 Imp. pints),
cooling system 11.1 litres (19.50 Imp. pints), fuel tank
61 litres (13.50 Imp. gal).
  Notes—Top speed 205 km/h (127 mph)

MORRIS MARINA 1.3 SL   1275 cm^3

Engine—water-cooled, 4-cylinder, in-line, front mounted, bore x stroke 70.1 x 81.28, displacement 1275 cm^3, ohv, compression ratio 8.8:1, max. power 42 kW (57 bhp) at 5500/min, max. torque 93 Nm (69 lbf.ft) at 2450/min, 1 SU carburettor.
Transmission—rear wheels; 4-speed gearbox.
Steering—rack and pinion.
Suspension—front/rear independent wishbones with anti-roll bar, dead axle.
Springs—front: coil, rear: leaf springs, telescopic shock absorbers front and rear.
Brakes—front/rear discs/drums.
Dimensions and weights—length 4290mm, width 1660mm height 1420mm, wheelbase 2438mm, kerb weight 880 kg.
Tyres—145 SR 13.
Capacities—engine sump 4 litres (7 Imp. pints), cooling system 4.2 litres (7.50 Imp. pints), fuel tank 52 litres (11.50 Imp. gal).
  Notes—Top speed 132 km/h (82 mph).

114

OLDSMOBILE DELTA 88 ROYALE DIESEL   5737 cm^3

Engine—water-cooled, V8, diesel, front mounted,, bore x stroke 103 x 86, displacement 5737 cm^3, ohv, compression ratio 22.5:1, max. power 90 kW (122 bhp) at 3600/min, max. torque 298 Nm (220 lbf.ft) at 1600/min, fuel injection pump Stanadyne.
Transmission—rear wheels; automatic transmission.
Steering—recirculating ball, servo-assisted.
Suspension—front/rear independent wishbones with anti-roll bar, dead axle.
Springs—coil springs and telescopic shock absorbers front and rear.
Brakes—front/rear discs/drums, servo-assisted.
Dimensions and weights—length 5525mm, width 1950mm height 1385mm, wheelbase 2950mm, kerb weight 1811kg.
Tyres—GR 78-15.
Capacities—engine sump 7.7 litres (13.50 Imp. pints), cooling system 17 litres (30 Imp. pints), fuel tank 98 litres (21.50 Imp. gal).
    Notes—Top speed 160 km/h (99 mph).

OPEL KADETT 1.2S Berlina 1196 cm^3

Engine—water-cooled, 4-cylinder, in-line, front mounted, bore x stroke 79 x 61, displacement 1196 cm^3, ohv, compression ratio 9:1, max. power 44 kW (60 bhp) at 5400/min, max. torque 90 Nm (66 lbf.ft) at 3400/min, 1 Solex single carburettor.
Transmission—rear wheels; 4-speed gearbox.
Steering—rack and pinion.
Suspension—front/rear independent wishbones with anti-roll bar/dead axle with Panhard rod.
Springs—coil springs and telescopic shock absorbers front and rear.
Brakes—front/rear discs/drums, servo-assisted.
Dimensions and weights—length 4120mm, width 1580mm height 1310mm, wheelbase 2400mm, kerb weight 785 kg.
Tyres—155 SR 13.
Capacities—engine sump 2.75 litres (4.75 Imp. pints), cooling system 4.6 litres (8 Imp. pints), fuel tank 44 litres (9.75 Imp. gal).
  Notes—Top speed 142 km/h (88 mph).

OPEL ASCONA 1.6S   1584 cm^3

Engine—water-cooled, 4-cylinder, in-line, front mounted, bore x stroke 85 x 69.8, displacement 1584 cm^3, ohc, compression ratio 8.8:1, max. power 55 kW (75 bhp) at 5000/min, max. torque 115 Nm (85 lbf.ft) at 3800/min, 1 Solex single carburettor.
Transmission—rear wheels; 4-speed gearbox.
Seeering—rack and pinion.
Suspension—front/rear independent wishbones with anti-roll bar/dead axle with Panhard rod.
Springs—coil springs and telescopic shock absorbers front and rear.
Brakes—front/rear discs/drums, servo-assisted.
Dimensions and weights—length 4321mm, width 1670mm height 1380mm, wheelbase 2518mm, kerb weight 980 kg.
Tyres—165 SR 13.
Capacities—engine sump 3.8 litres (6.75 Imp. pints), cooling system 6.5 litres (11.50 Imp. pints), fuel tank 50 litres (11 Imp. gal).
  Notes—Top speed 158 km/h (98 mph).

OPEL ASCONA 2.0D   1998 cm^3

Engine—water-cooled, 4-cylinder, in-line, diesel, front
mounted, bore x stroke 86.5 x 85, displacement 1998 cm^3
ohv, compression ratio 22:1, max. power 43 kW (58 bhp)
at 4200/min, max. torque 115 Nm (85 lbf.ft) at 2400/min,
Bosch fuel injection pump.
Transmission—rear wheels; 4-speed gearbox.
Steering—rack and pinion.
Suspension—front/rear independent wishbones with anti-
roll bar/dead axle with Panhard rod.
Springs—coil springs and telescopic shock absorbers front
and rear.
Brakes—front/rear discs/drums, servo-assisted.
Dimensions and weights—length 4321mm, width 1670mm
height 1380mm, wheelbase 2518mm, kerb weight 1080kg.
Tyres—165 SR 13.
Capacities—engine sump 5.5 litres (9.75 Imp. pints), cooling
system 11.2 litres (19.75 Imp. pints), fuel tank 50 litres
(11 Imp. gal).
   Notes—Top speed 137 km/h (85 mph).

OPEL MANTA Coupe Berlinetta 2.0S 1979 cm^3

Engine—water-cooled, 4-cylinder, in-line, front mounted, bore x stroke 95 x 69.8, displacement 1979 cm^3, ohc, compression ratio 9:1, max. power 74 kW (101 bhp) at 5400/min, max. torque 153 Nm (113 lbf.ft) at 3800/min, 1 GMF Varajet II carburettor.
Transmission—rear wheels; 4-speed gearbox.
Steering—rack and pinion.
Suspension—front/rear independent wishbone with anti-roll bar/dead axle with Panhard rod.
Springs—coil springs and telescopic shock absorbers front and rear.
Brakes—front/rear discs/drums, servo-assisted.
Dimensions and weights—length 4376mm, width 1670mm height 1340mm, wheelbase 2518mm, kerb weight 1030kg.
Tyres—165 SR 13.
Capacities—engine sump 3.8 litres (6.75 Imp. pints), cooling system 6.2 litres (11 Imp. pints), fuel tank 50 litres (11 Imp. gal).
 Notes—Top speed 180 km/h (112 mph).

OPEL REKORD 2.0E
De LUXE BERLINA   1956 cm³

Engine—water-cooled, 4-cylinder, in-line, front mounted, bore x stroke 95 x 69.8, displacement 1956 cm³, ohc, compression ratio 9.4:1, max. power 81 kW (110 bhp) at 5400/min, max. torque 162 Nm (120 lbf.ft) at 3000/min.

Transmission—rear wheels; 4-speed gearbox.

Steering—recirculating ball.

Suspension—front/rear McPherson struts with anti-roll bar/dead axle with Panhard rod.

Springs—coil springs and telescopic shock absorbers front and rear.

Brakes—front/rear discs/drums, servo-assisted.

Dimensions and weights—length 4593mm, width 1726mm height 1420mm, wheelbase 2660mm, kerb weight 1120kg.

Tyres—175 HR 14.

Capacities—engine sump 3.8 litres (6.75 Imp. pints), cooling system 9.1 litres (16 Imp. pints), fuel tank 65 litres (14.25 Imp. gal).

   Notes—Top speed 179 km/h (111 mph).

OPEL REKORD 2.3D Caravan DeLuxe 2260 cm^3

Engine—water-cooled, 4-cylinder, in-line, diesel, front mounted, bore x stroke 92 x 85, displacement 2260 cm^3 ohc, compression ratio 22:1, max. power 48 kW (65 bhp) at 4200/min, max. torque 127 Nm (94 lbf.ft) at 2500/min, Bosch fuel injection pump.
Transmission—rear wheels; 4-speed gearbox.
Steering—recirculating ball.
Suspension—front/rear McPherson struts with anti-roll bar/dead axle with Panhard rod.
Springs—coil springs and telescopic shock absorbers front and rear.
Brakes—front/rear discs/drums, servo-assisted.
Dimensions and weights—length 4620mm, width 1726mm height 1470mm, wheelbase 2668mm, kerb weight 1170kg.
Tyres—175 SR 13.
Capacities—engine sump 5.5 litres (9.75 Imp. pints), cooling system 11.5 litres (20.25 Imp. pints), fuel tank 65 litres (14.25 Imp. gal).
  Notes—Top speed 137 km/h (85 mph).

OPEL SENATOR 3.0E CD
2968 cm^3

Engine—water-cooled, 6-cylinder, in-line, front mounted, bore x stroke 95 x 69.8, displacement 2968 cm^3, 1 ohc, compression ratio 9.4:1, max. power 132 kW (179 bhp) at 5800/min, max. torque 243 Nm (179 lbf.ft) at 4800/min, fuel injection Bosch L-Jetronic.

Transmission—rear wheels; automatic transmission.

Steering—recirculating ball, servo-assisted.

Suspension—front/rear McPherson struts with anti-roll bar/independent transversal trailing arms.

Springs—coil springs and telescopic shock absorbers front and rear.

Brakes—front/rear discs/discs servo-assisted.

Dimensions and weights—length 4811mm, width 1728 mm, height 1415mm, wheelbase 2683mm, kerb weight 1370kg.

Tyres—195/70 VR 14.

Capacities—engine sump 5.5 litres (9.75 Imp. pints), cooling system 9.8 litres (17.25 Imp. pints), fuel tank 75 litres (16.50 Imp. gal).

Notes—Top speed 205 km/h (127 mph)

PEUGEOT 104 GL6   1124 cm^3

Engine—water-cooled, 4-cylinder, in-line, front mounted, bore x stroke 72 x 69, displacement 1124 cm^3, ohc, compression ratio 9.2:1, max. power 42 kW (57 bhp) at 6000/min, max. torque 81 Nm (60 lbf.ft) at 3000/min, 1 Solex single carburettor.
Transmission—front wheels; 4-speed gearbox.
Steering—rack and pinion.
Suspension—front/rear McPherson struts with independent trailing arms.
Springs—coil springs and telescopic shock absorbers front and rear.
Brakes—front/rear discs/drums.
Dimensions and weights—length 3582mm, width 1522mm height 1402mm, wheelbase 2420mm, kerb weight 790 kg.
Tyres—135 SR 13.
Capacities—engine sump 4.5 litres (8 Imp. pints), cooling system 5.6 litres (9.75 Imp. pints), fuel tank 40 litres (8.75 Imp. gal).
  Notes—Top speed 145 km/h (90 mph).

PEUGEOT 304 GLD ESTATE 1357 cm^3

Engine—water-cooled, 4-cylinder, in-line, diesel, front mounted, bore x stroke 78 x 71, displacement 1357 cm^3 ohc, compression ratio 23.3:1, max. power 33.1 kW (45 bhp) at 5000/min, max. torque 77 Nm (57 lbf.ft) at 2500/min, Bosch injection equipment.
Transmission—front wheels; 4-speed gearbox.
Steering—rack and pinion.
Suspension—front/rear McPherson struts/independent trailing arms.
Springs—coil springs and telescopic shock absorbers front and rear.
Brakes—front/rear discs/drums, servo-assisted.
Dimensions and weights—length 4010mm, width 1570 mm, height 1430mm, wheelbase 2590mm, kerb weight 970 kg.
Tyres—145 SR 14.
Capacities—engine sump 5 litres (8.75 Imp. pints), cooling system 6.5 litres (14.50 Imp. pints), fuel tank 42 litres (9.25 Imp. gal).
 Notes—Top speed 130 km/h (81 mph).

PEUGEOT 305 SR 1472 cm^3

Engine—water-cooled, 4-cylinder, in-line, front mounted, bore x stroke 78 x 77, displacement 1472 cm^3, ohc, compression ratio 9.2:1, max. power 54 kW (74 bhp) at 6000/min, max. torque 116 Nm (86 lbf.ft) at 3000/min, 1 single Solex carburettor.
Transmission—front wheels; 4-speed gearbox.
Steering—rack and pinion.
Suspension—Front/rear McPherson struts/independent trailing arms.
Springs—coil springs and telescopic shock absorbers front and rear.
Brakes—front/rear discs/drums, servo-assisted.
Dimensions and weights—length 4237mm, width 1630 mm, height 1400mm, wheelbase 2620mm, kerb weight 940 kg.
Tyres—145 SR 14.
Capacities—engine sump 4 litres (7 Imp. pints), cooling system 5.8 litres (10.25 Imp. pints), fuel tank 43 litres (9.50 Imp. gal).

   Notes—Top speed 153 km/h (95 mph)

PEUGEOT 504 GL $1971\ cm^3$

Engine—water-cooled, 4-cylinder, in-line, front mounted, bore x stroke 88 x 81, displacement 1971 cm^3, ohv, compression ratio 8.8:1, max. power 71 kW (96 bhp) at 5200/min, max. torque 161 Nm (119 lbf.ft) at 3000/min 1 double choke Zenith carburettor.

Transmission—rear wheels, automatic transmission or 4-speed gearbox.

Steering—rack and pinion. Servo-assisted.

Suspension—front/rear McPherson struts/independent trailing arms.

Springs—coil springs and telescopic shock absorbers front and rear.

Brakes—front/rear discs/drums, servo-assisted.

Dimensions and weights—length 4490mm, width 1690 mm, height 1460mm, wheelbase 2740mm, kerb weight 1230 kg.

Tyres—175 SR 14.

Capacities—engine sump 4 litres (7 Imp. pints), cooling system 7.8 litres (13.75 Imp. pints), fuel tank 56 litres (12.25 Imp. gal).

　Notes—Top speed 164 km/h (102 mph).

PEUGEOT 504 GLD FAMILIALE   2304 cm^3

Engine—water-cooled, 4-cylinder, in-line, diesel, front mounted, bore x stroke 94 x 83, displacement 2304 cm^3 ohv, compression ratio 22.2:1, max. power 52 kW (70 bhp) at 4500/min, max. torque 131 Nm (96 lbf.ft) at 2000/min, Rotor diesel injection equipment.
Transmission—rear wheels; 4-speed gearbox
Steering—rack and pinion. Servo-assisted.
Suspension—front/rear McPherson struts/independent trailing arms.
Springs—coil springs and telescopic shock absorbers front and rear.
Brakes—front/rear discs/drums, servo-assisted.
Dimensions and weights—length 4800mm, width 1690mm height 1550mm, wheelbase 2900mm, kerb weight 1410 kg.
Tyres—185 SR 14.
Capacities—engine sump 5 litres (8.75 Imp. pints), cooling system 10 litres (17.50 Imp. pints), fuel tank 60 litres (13.25 Imp. gal).
  Notes—Top speed 130 km/h (81 mph).

PEUGEOT 504 Cabriolet   1971 cm^3

Engine—water-cooled, 4-cylinder, in-line, front mounted, bore x stroke 88 x 81, displacement 1971 cm^3, ohv, compression ratio 8.8:1, max. power 78 kW (106 bhp) at 5200/min, max. torque 169 Nm (125 lbf.ft) at 3000/min, Kugelfischer fuel injection.
Transmission—rear wheels; 4-speed gearbox.
Steering—rack and pinion.
Suspension—front/rear McPherson struts with anti-roll bar, independent transversal trailing arms.
Springs—coil springs and telescopic shock absorbers front and rear.
Brakes—front/rear:discs/discs servo-assisted.
Dimensions and weights—length 4360mm, width 1700mm height 1360mm, wheelbase 2550mm, kerb weight 1235kg.
Tyres—175 HR 14.
Capacities—engine sump 4 litres (7 Imp. pints), cooling system 7.8 litres (13.75 Imp. pints), fuel tank 56 litres (12.25 Imp. gal).
  Notes—Top speed 179 km/h (111 mph).

PEUGEOT 604 TI   2664 cm^3

Engine—water-cooled, V6, front mounted, bore x stroke 88 x 73, displacement 2664 cm^3, 2 ohc, compression ratio 8.65:1, max. power 106 kW (144 bhp) at 5500/min max. torque 217 Nm (160 lbf.ft) at 3000/min, Bosch K— Jetronic fuel injection.
Transmission—rear wheels; 5-speed gearbox.
Steering—rack and pinion, servo-assisted.
Suspension—front/rear McPherson struts with anti-roll bar/independent trailing arms.
Springs—coil springs and telescopic shock absorbers front and rear.
Brakes—front/rear:discs/discs servo assisted.
Dimensions and weights—length 4721mm, width 1770 mm, height 1435mm, wheelbase 2800mm, kerb weight 1410kg.
Tyres—175 HR 14.
Capacities—engine sump 6 litres (10.50 Imp. pints), cooling system 10.3 litres (18 Imp. pints), fuel tank 70 litres (15.50 Imp. gal).
   Notes—Top speed 185 km/h (115 mph)

PLYMOUTH VOLARE PREMIER 5210 cm³

Engine—water-cooled, V8, front mounted, bore x stroke 99.31 x 84.07, displacement 5210 cm³, ohv, compression ratio 8.5:1, max. power 114 kW (155 bhp) at 4000/min, max. torque 388 Nm (286 lbf.ft) at 1600/min, 1 Carter double carburettor.

Transmission—rear wheels; automatic transmission Chrysler.

Steering—recirculating ball, servo-assisted.

Suspension—front/rear independent wishbones with anti-roll bar, dead axle.

Springs—front: transversal torsion bars, rear: transversal learf springs, telescopic shock absorbers front and rear.

Brakes—front/rear discs/drums, servo-assisted.

Dimensions and weights—length 5110mm, width 1860mm height 1400mm, wheelbase 2860mm, kerb weight 1820kg.

Tyres—ER 78-14.

Capacities—engine sump 4.7 litres (8.25 Imp. pints), cooling system 15.7 litres (27.50 Imp. pints) fuel tank 68 litres (15 Imp. gal).

Notes—Top speed 170 km/h (105 mph).

POLSKI-FIAT POLONEZ   1481 cm^3

Engine—water-cooled, 4-cylinder, in-line, front mounted, bore x stroke 77 x 79.5, displacement 1481 cm^3, ohv, compression ratio 9.5:1, max. power 60 kW (82 bhp) at 5200/min, max. torque 113 Nm (83 lbf.ft) at 3400/min, 1 Weber carburettor.
Transmission—rear wheels; 4-speed gearbox.
Steering—rack and pinion.
Suspension—front/rear independent wishbones with anti-roll bar, dead axle.
Springs—front: coil springs, rear: leaf springs, telescopic shock absorbers front and rear.
Brakes—front/rear discs, servo-assisted.
Dimensions and weights—length 4272mm, width 1650mm height 1379mm, wheelbase 2509mm, kerb weight 1140kg.
Tyres—175 SR 13.
Capacities—engine sump 3.5 litres (6 Imp. pints), cooling system 7.5 litres (13.25 Imp. pints), fuel tank 45 litres (10 Imp. gal).
  Notes—Top speed 155 km/h (96 mph).

PONTIAC SUNBIRD SPORT SAFARI 3791 cm^3

Engine—water-cooled, V6, front mounted, bore x stroke 96.52 x 86.36, displacement 3791 cm^3, ohv, compression ratio 8.0:1, max. power 78 kW (106 bhp) at 3400/min, max. torque 251 Nm (185 lbf.ft) at 2000/min,1 Rochester double carburettor.
Transmission—rear wheels; automatic transmission.
Steering—recirculating ball.
Suspension—front/rear independent wishbones with anti-roll bar/dead axle with Panhard rod.
Springs—coil springs and telescopic shock absorbers front and rear.
Brakes—front/rear discs/drums, servo-assisted.
Dimensions and weights—length 4515mm, width 1660mm height 1265mm, wheelbase 2465mm, kerb weight 1445kg.
Tyres—BR 78-13.
Capacities—engine sump 4.7 litres (8.25 Imp. pints), cooling system 11.4 litres (20 Imp. pints), fuel tank 70 litres (15.50 Imp. gal).
 Notes—Top speed 175 km/h (109 mph).

PONTIAC FIREBIRD FORMULA   6561 cm^3

Engine—water-cooled, V8, front mounted, bore x stroke 104.68 x 95.25, displacement 6561 cm^3, ohv, compression ratio 7.6:1, max. power 132 kW (179 bhp) at 3600/min, max. torque 440 Nm (325 lbf.ft) at 1600/min, 1 Rochester carburettor.
Transmission—rear wheels; automatic transmission.
Steering—recirculating ball, servo-assisted.
Suspension—front/rear independent wishbone with anti-roll bar/dead axle.
Springs—front: coil springs, rear: leaf springs, telescopic shock absorbers front and rear.
Brakes—front/rear discs/drums, servo-assisted.
Dimensions and weights—length 4999mm, width 1854mm height 1300mm, wheelbase 2745mm, kerb weight 1720kg.
Tyres—GR 70-15.
Capacities—engine sump 4.6 litres (8 Imp. pints), cooling system 17.4 litres (30.50 Imp. pints), fuel tank 79 litres (17.25 Imp. gal).
  Notes—Top speed 190 km/h (118 mph).

PORSCHE 924   1984 cm^3

Engine—water-cooled, 4-cylinder, in-line, front mounted, bore x stroke 86.5 x 84.4, displacement 1984 cm^3, ohc, compression ratio 9.3:1, max. power 92 kW (125 bhp) at 5800/min, max. torque 165 Nm (122 lbf.ft) at 3500/min Bosch K-Jetronic fuel injection.
Transmission—rear wheels; 5-speed gearbox.
Steering—rack and pinion.
Suspension—front/rear McPherson struts, independent trailing arms.
Springs—coil springs and telescopic shock absorbers front and rear.
Brakes—front/rear:discs/drums, servo-assisted.
Dimensions and weights—length 4200mm, width 1685 mm, height 1270mm, wheelbase 2400mm, kerb weight 1080 kg.
Tyres—165 HR 14.
Capacities—engine sump 5 litres (8.75 Imp. pints), cooling system 8 litres (14 Imp. pints), fuel tank 62 litres (13.50 Imp. gal).
   Notes—Top speed 200 km/h (124 mph)

PORSCHE 911SC   2994 cm^3

Engine—air-cooled, 6-cylinder, flat engine, rear mounted, bore x stroke 95 x 70.4, displacement 2994 cm^3, dohc, compression ratio 8.5:1, max. power 132 kW (179 bhp) at 5500/min, max. torque 265 Nm (196 lbf.ft) at 4200/min, Bosch K-Jetronic fuel injection.
Transmission—rear wheels; 5-speed gearbox.
Steering—rack and pinion.
Suspension—front/rear McPherson struts with anti-roll bar, independent trailing arms.
Springs—coil springs and telescopic shock absorbers front and rear.
Brakes—front/rear discs/discs servo-assisted.
Dimensions and weights—length 4291mm, width 1652mm, height 1320mm, wheelbase 2272mm, kerb weight 1160kg.
Tyres—front: 185/70 VR 15, rear: 215/60 VR 15.
Capacities—engine sump 13 litres (23 Imp. pints), fuel tank 80 litres (17.50 Imp. gal).
  Notes—Top speed 220 km/h (137 mph).

PORSCHE 928   4474 cm^3

Engine—water-cooled, V8, front mounted, bore x stroke 95 x 78.9, displacement 4474 cm^3, 2 ohc, compression ratio 8.5:1, max. power 177 kW (241 bhp) at 5500/min, max. torque 350 Nm (258 lbf.ft) at 3600/min, Bosch K-Jetronic fuel injection.
Transmission—rear wheels; 5-speed gearbox.
Steering—rack and pinion, servo-assisted.
Suspension—front/rear independent wishbones with anti-roll bar/independent transversal trailing arms.
Springs—coil springs and telescopic shock absorbers front and rear.
Brakes—front/rear discs/discs servo-assisted.
Dimensions and weights—length 4447mm, width 1836 mm, height 1313mm, wheelbase 2500mm, kerb weight 1450 kg.
Tyres—225/50 VR 16.
Capacities—engine sump 6.5 litres (11.50 Imp. pints), cooling system 6 litres (10.50 Imp. pints), fuel tank 86 litres (19 Imp. gal).
  Notes—Top speed 230 km/h (143 mph)

PRINCESS 2000 HL   1993 cm^3

Engine—water-cooled, 4-cylinder, in-line, front mounted, bore x stroke 84.45 x 89, displacement 1993 cm^3, ohc, compression ratio 9:1, max. power 69 kW (94 bhp) at 4900/min, max. torque 153 Nm (113 lbf.ft) at 3400/min, 1 SU carburettor.
Transmission—front wheels; 4-speed gearbox.
Steering—rack and pinion, servo-assisted.
Suspension—front/rear independent wishbones, independent trailing arms.
Springs—"Hydragas" system front and rear.
Brakes—front/rear discs/drums, servo-assisted.
Dimensions and weights—length 4455mm, width 1730mm height 1409mm, wheelbase 2680mm, kerb weight 1160kg.
Tyres—185/70 SR 14.
Capacities—engine sump 5.8 litres (10.25 Imp. pints), cooling system 6 litres (10.50 Imp. pints), fuel tank 73 litres (16 Imp. gal).
   Notes—Top speed 160 km/h (99 mph).

RELIANT KITTEN DL   848 cm^3

Engine—water-cooled, 4-cylinder, in-line, front mounted, bore x stroke 62.5 x 69.09, displacement 848 cm^3, compression ratio 9.5:1, max. power 30 kW (41 bhp) at 5500/min, max. torque 62.8 Nm (46 lbf.ft) at 3500/min 1 SU carburettor.

Transmission—rear wheels; 4-speed gearbox.

Steering—rack and pinion.

Suspension—front/rear independent wishbones with anti-roll bar, dead axle.

Springs—front: coil springs, rear leaf springs, telescopic shock absorbers front and rear.

Brakes—front/rear drums/drums.

Dimensions and weights—length 3327mm, width 1422mm height 1397mm, wheelbase 2146mm, kerb weight 505 kg.

Tyres—145 SR 10.

Capacities—engine sump 3.1 litres (5.50 Imp. pints), cooling system 3.7 litres (6.50 Imp. pints), fuel tank 27.3 litres (6 Imp. gal).

Notes—Top speed 128 km/h (79 mph).

RELIANT SCIMITAR GTE $2994\ cm^3$

Engine—water-cooled, V6, front mounted, bore x stroke 93.67 x 72.42, displacement 2994 cm^3, 1 ohv, compression ratio 8.9:1, max. power 99.4 kW (135 bhp) at 5500/min, max. torque 235 Nm (173 lbf.ft) at 3000/min, 1 single carburettor.
Transmission—rear wheels; 4-speed gearbox.
Steering—rack and pinion, servo-assisted.
Suspension—front/rear independent wishbones with anti-roll bar/dead axle.
Springs—coil springs and telescopic shock absorbers front and rear.
Brakes—front/rear discs/drums, servo-assisted.
Dimensions and weights—length 4440mm, width 1710 mm, height 1320mm, wheelbase 2630mm, kerb weight 1290 kg.
Tyres—185 HR 14.
Capacities—engine sump 5.4 litres (9.50 Imp. pints), cooling system 11.3 litres (20 Imp. pints), fuel tank 90 litres (20 Imp. gal).
  Notes—Top speed 190 km/h (118 mph)

RENAULT 4GTL 1108 cm^3

Engine—water-cooled, 4-cylinder, in-line, front mounted, bore x stroke 70 x 72, displacement 1108 cm^3, ohv, compression ratio 9.5:1, max. power 25 kW (34 bhp) at 4000/min, max. torque 75 Nm (55 lbf.ft) at 2500/min, 1 Solex carburettor.

Transmission—front wheels; 4-speed gearbox.

Steering—rack and pinion.

Suspension—front/rear independent wishbones with anti-roll bar, independent trailing arms.

Springs—front: longitudinal torsion bars, rear transversal torsion bars, telescopic shock absorbers front and rear.

Brakes—front/rear discs/drums, servo-assisted.

Dimensions and weights—length 3670mm, width 1510mm height 1550mm, wheelbase left 2400 mm, right 2450mm, kerb weight 720 kg.

Tyres— 135 SR 13.

Capacities—engine sump 3 litres (5.25 Imp. pints), cooling system 5.9 litres (10.25 Imp. pints), fuel tank 34 litres (7.50 Imp. gal).

　Notes—Top speed 122 km/h (76 mph).

RENAULT 5 AUTOMATIC 1300   1289 cm^3

Engine—water-cooled, 4-cylinder, in-line, front mounted, bore x stroke 73 x 77, displacement 1289 cm^3, ohv, compression ratio 9.5:1, max. power 41 kW (56 bhp) at 5750/min, max. torque 94 Nm (69 lbf.ft) at 2500/min, 1 Solex double carburettor.
Transmission—front wheels; Renault automatic transmission. Renault.
Steering—rack and pinion.
Suspension—front/rear independent wishbones with anti-roll bar/independent transversal trailing arms.
Springs—telescopic shock absorbers front and rear.
Brakes—front/rear discs/drums, servo-assisted.
Dimensions and weights—length 3516mm, width 1549 mm, height 1315mm, wheelbase 2404mm, kerb weight 810 kg.
Tyres—145 SR13.
Capacties—engine sump 3.5 litres (6.25 Imp. pints), cooling system 6.3 litres (11 Imp. pints), fuel tank 38 litres (8.25 Imp. gal).
  Notes—Top speed 140 km/h (87 mph)

RENAULT 6 TL 1108 cm^3

Engine—water-cooled, 4-cylinder, in-line, front mounted, bore x stroke 70 x 72, displacement 1108 cm^3, ohv, compression ratio 9.5:1, max. power 35 kW (48 bhp) at 5300/min, max. torque 78 Nm (58 lbf.ft) at 3000/min, 1 Zenith carburettor.

Transmission—front wheels; 4-speed gearbox.

Steering—rack and pinion.

Suspension—front/rear: independent wishbones with anti-roll bar, independent trailing arms.

Springs—Telescopic shock absorbers front and rear.

Brakes—front/rear discs/drums.

Dimensions and weights—length 3860mm, width 1510mm height 1480mm, wheelbase left 2400 mm, right 2450mm, kerb weight 820 kg.

Tyres—145 SR 13.

Capacities—engine sump 3.3 litres (5.75 Imp. pints), cooling system 6.3 litres (11 Imp. pints), fuel tank 40 litres (8.75 Imp. gal).

   Notes—Top speed 135 km/h (84 mph).

RENAULT 12TL   1289 cm^3

Engine—water-cooled, 4-cylinder, in-line, front mounted,
bore x stroke 73 x 77, displacement 1289 cm^3, ohv,
compression ratio 9.5:1, max. power 40 kW (54 bhp) at
5250/min, max. torque 88 Nm (65 lbf.ft) at 3500/min,
1 Solex carburettor.
Transmission—front wheels; 4-speed gearbox.
Steering—rack and pinion.
Suspension—front/rear independent wishbones with anti-
roll bar, independent trailing arms.
Springs—coil springs and telescopic shock absorbers front
and rear.
Brakes—front/rear discs/drums, servo-assisted.
Dimensions and weights—length 4348mm, width 1616mm
height 1435mm, wheelbase 2440mm, kerb weight 860 kg.
Tyres—145 SR 13.
Capacities—engine sump 3.3 litres (5.75 Imp. pints),
cooling system 5 litres (8.75 Imp. pints), fuel tank 47
litres (10.25 Imp. gal).
  Notes—Top speed 140 km/h (87 mph).

RENAULT 14 TS 1218 cm^3

Engine—water-cooled, 4-cylinder, in-line, front mounted, bore x stroke 75 x 69, displacement 1218 cm^3, ohv, compression ratio 9.3:1, max. power 51 kW (69 bhp) at 6000/min, max. torque 92 Nm (68 lbf.ft) at 3000/min, 1 Solex carburettor.

Transmission—front wheels; 4-speed gearbox.

Steering—rack and pinion.

Suspension—front/rear independent wishbones with anti-roll bar, independent transversal trailing arms.

Springs—coil springs and telescopic shock absorbers front and rear.

Brakes—front/rear discs/drums, servo-assisted.

Dimensions and weights—length 4025mm, width 1624mm height 1405mm, wheelbase left 2530mm, right 2498mm, kerb weight 865 kg.

Tyres—145 SR 13.

Capacities—engine sump 4.3 litres (7.50 Imp. pints), cooling system 6 litres (10.50 Imp. pints), fuel tank 48 litres (10.50 Imp. gal).

  Notes—Top speed 155 km/h (96 mph).

RENAULT 15 GTL

1289 cm^3

Engine—water-cooled, 4-cylinder, in-line, front mounted, bore x stroke 73 x 77, displacement 1289 cm^3, ohv, compression ratio 9.5:1, max. power 44 kW (60 bhp) at 5500/min, max. torque 91 Nm (67 lbf.ft) at 3500/min, 1 Weber double carburettor.
Transmission—front wheels; 4-speed gearbox.
Steering—rack and pinion.
Suspension—front/rear independent wishbones with anti-roll bar, independent trailing arms.
Springs—coil springs and telescopic shock absorbers front and rear.
Brakes—front/rear discs/drums, servo-assisted.
Dimensions and weights—length 4260mm, width 1630mm height 1340mm, wheelbase 2440mm, kerb weight 920kg.
Tyres—145 SR 13.
Capacities—engine sump 3.3 litres (5.75 Imp. pints), cooling system 5 litres (8.75 Imp. pints), fuel tank 55 litres (12 Imp. gal).
  Notes—Top speed 148 km/h (92 mph).

RENAULT 16 TX

1647 cm^3

Engine—water-cooled, 4-cylinder, in-line, front mounted,
bore x stroke 79 x 84, displacement 1647 cm^3, ohv,
compression ratio 9.25:1, max. power 66 kW (90 bhp) at
6000/min, max. torque 130 Nm (96 lbf.ft) at 4000/min,
1 Weber carburettor.

Transmission—front wheels; 5-speed gearbox.

Steering—rack and pinion.

Suspension—front/rear independent wishbones with anti-
roll bar, independent trailing arms.

Springs—coil springs and telescopic shock absorbers front
and rear.

Brakes—front/rear discs/drums, servo-assisted.

Dimensions and weights—length 4237mm, width 1630mm
height 1450mm, wheelbase left 2720mm, right 2650mm,
kerb weight 1065 kg.

Tyres—155 SR 14.

Capacities—engine sump 4.3 litres (7.50 Imp. pints),
cooling system 6.8 litres (12 Imp. pints), fuel tank 50
litres (11 Imp. gal).

   Notes—Top speed 165 km/h (102 mph).

RENAULT 18 TS $1647\ cm^3$

Engine—water-cooled, 4-cylinder, in-line, front mounted, bore x stroke 79 x 84, displacement 1647 cm^3, ohv, compression ratio 9.3:1, max. power 58 kW (79 bhp) at 5500/min, max. torque 123 Nm (91 lbf.ft) at 3000/min, 1 Solex single carburettor.
Transmission—front wheels; 4-speed gearbox.
Steering—rack and pinion.
Suspension—front/rear independent wishbones with anti-roll bar, independent trailing arms.
Springs—coil springs and telescopic shock absorbers front and rear.
Brakes—front/rear discs/drums, servo-assisted.
Dimensions and weights—length 4369mm, width 1689 mm, height 1405mm, wheelbase 2441mm, kerb weight 940 kg.
Tyres—155 SR13.
Capacities—engine sump 3 litres (5.25 Imp. pints), cooling system 6 litres (10.50 Imp. pints), fuel tank 53 litres (11.50 Imp. gal).
  Notes—Top speed 163 km/h (101 mph)

RENAULT 20 TS

1995 cm^3

Engine—water-cooled, 4-cylinder, in-line, front mounted,
bore x stroke 88 x 82, displacement 1995 cm^3, ohc,
compression ratio 9.2:1, max. power 80 kW (109 bhp)
at 5500/min, max. torque 167 Nm (123 lbf.ft) at 3000/
min, 1 Weber double carburettor.
Transmission—front wheels; 4-speed gearbox.
Steering—rack and pinion, servo-assisted.
Suspension—independent wishbones with anti-roll bars.
Springs—coil springs and telescopic shock absorbers front
and rear.
Brakes—front/rear discs/drums, servo-assisted.
Dimensions and weights—length 4520mm, width 1726mm
height 1438mm, wheelbase 2671mm, kerb weight 1260kg.
Tyres—165 SR 14.
Capacities—engine sump 5.3 litres (9.25 Imp. pints),
cooling system 9.8 litres (17.25 Imp. pints), fuel tank
67 litres (14.75 Imp. gal).
   Notes—Top speed 170 km/h (105 mph).

ROLLS-ROYCE SILVER SHADOW II   6750 cm^3

Engine—water-cooled, V8-cylinder, front mounted, bore x stroke 104.1 x 99.1, displacement 6750 cm^3, 1 ohv, compression ratio 8:1, max. power and torque figures not given. 2 SU carburettors.
Transmission—rear wheels; automatic transmission GM.
Steering—rack and pinion, servo-assisted.
Suspension—front/rear independent wishbones with anti-roll bar, independent wishbones and automatic levelling control.
Springs—coil springs and telescopic shock absorbers front and rear.
Brakes—front/rear discs, servo-assisted.
Dimensions and weights—length 5170mm, width 1800 mm, height 1520mm, wheelbase 3040mm, kerb weight 2136 kg.
Tyres—235/70 HR x 15.
Capacities—engine sump 8 litres (14 Imp. pints), cooling system 16 litres (28 Imp. pints), fuel tank 107 litres (23.50 Imp. gal).
  Notes—Top speed 190 km/h (118 mph)

ROVER 2600   2597cm^3

Engine—water-cooled, 6-cylinder, in-line, front mounted, bore x stroke 81 x 89, displacement 2597 cm^3, 1 ohc, compression ratio 9.25:1, max. power 101,4 kW (138 bhp) at 5000/min, max. torque 206 Nm (152 lbf.ft) at 3750/min, 2SU carburettors.
Transmission—rear wheels; 5-speed gearbox.
Steering—rack and pinion, servo-assisted.
Suspension—front/rear McPherson struts, with anti-roll bar, dead axle.
Springs—coil springs and telescopic shock absorbers front and rear.
Brakes—front/rear discs/drums, servo-assisted.
Dimensions and weights—length 4698mm, width 1769mm height 1354mm, wheelbase 2815mm, kerb weight 1350kg.
Tyres—175 HR 14.
Capacities—engine sump 7.1 litres (12.50 Imp. pints), cooling system 8.8 litres (15.50 Imp. pints), fuel tank 65.9 litres (14.50 Imp. gal).

  Notes—Top speed 192 km/h (119 mph)

RANGE ROVER 3528 cm^3

Engine—water-cooled, V8-cylinder, front mounted, bore x stroke 88.9 x 71.12, displacement 3528 cm^3, ohv, compression ratio 8.25:1, max. power 97 kW (132 bhp) at 5000/min, max. torque 2511 Nm (185 lbf.ft) at 2500/min, 2 SV carburettors.
Transmission—all wheels; 4-speed gearbox, with two-speed transfer box and overdrive.
Steering—recirculating ball, servo-assisted.
Suspension—front/rear. Dead axles with Panhard rod.
Springs—coil springs and telescopic shock absorbers front and rear.
Brakes—front/rear discs/discs, servo-assisted.
Dimensions and weights—length 4470mm, width 1780mm height 1780mm, wheelbase 2540mm, kerb weight 1724kg.
Tyres—205 SR 16.
Capacities—engine sump 5.7 litres (10 Imp. pints), cooling system 11.3 litres (20 Imp. pints), fuel tank 86 litres (19 Imp. gal).
Notes—Top speed 154 km/h (95 mph)

RUSKA GURGEL JEEP X 12   1596 cm^3

Engine—air-cooled, 4-cylinder, flat engine, rear mounted, bore x stroke 86 x 69, displacement 1596 cm^3, ohv, compression ratio 7.5:1, max. power 37 kW (50 bhp) at 4000/min, max. torque 87 Nm (64 lbf.ft) at 3000/min, 1 Solex carburettor.
Transmission—rear wheels, 4-speed gearbox.
Steering—worm and roller.
Suspension—front/rear independent wishbones with anti-roll bar, independent trailing arms.
Springs—coil springs and telescopic shock absorbers front and rear.
Brakes—front/rear:drums/drums.
Dimensions and weights—length 3310mm, width 1590mm, height 1530mm, wheelbase 2040mm, kerb weight 850 kg.
Tyres—7.35 X 15.
Capacities—engine sump 2.5 litres (4.50 Imp. pints), fuel tank 38 litres (8.25 Imp. gal).
  Notes—Top speed 140 km/h (87 mph)

SAAB 99GL CM4   1985 cm^3

Engine—water-cooled, 4-cylinder, in-line, front mounted, bore x stroke 90 x 78, displacement 1985 cm^3, ohc, compression ratio 9.2:1, max. power 73.6 kW (100 bhp) at 5200/min, max. torque 161.8 Nm (126 lbf.ft) at 3500/min, 1 Zenith/Stromberg single carburettor.
Transmission—front wheels; 4-speed gearbox.
Steering—rack and pinion.
Suspension—front/rear independent wishbones, dead axle with Panhard rod.
Springs—coil springs and telescopic shock absorbers front and rear.
Brakes—front/rear discs/discs servo-assisted.
Dimensions and weights—length 4420mm, width 1690mm height 1440mm, wheelbase 2473mm, kerb weight 1220kg.
Tyres—165 SR 15.
Capacities—engine sump 3.5 litres (6.25 Imp. pints), cooling system 8 litres (14 Imp. pints), fuel tank 55 litres (12 Imp. gal).
  Notes—Top speed 162 km/h (101 mph).

SAAB 900 TURBO
1985 cm^3

Engine—water-cooled, 4-cylinder, in-line, front mounted,
bore x stroke 90 x 78, displacement 1985 cm^3, ohc,
compression ratio 7.2:1, max. power 106.5 kW (145 bhp)
at 5000/min, max. torque 235 Nm (173 lbf.ft) at 3000/
min, Bosch K-Jetronic fuel injection, turbo charged.
Transmission—front wheels; 4-speed gearbox.
Steering—rack and pinion.
Suspension—front/rear independent wishbones, dead
axle.
Springs—coil springs and telescopic shock absorbers front
and rear.
Brakes—front/rear discs/discs servo-assisted.
Dimensions and weights—length 4710mm, width 1690mm
height 1440mm, wheelbase 2525mm, kerb weight 1220kg.
Tyres—175/70 HR 15.
Capacities—engine sump 3.5 litres (6.25 Imp. pints),
cooling system 8 litres (14 Imp. pints), fuel tank 55 litres
(12 Imp. gal).
  Notes—Top speed 198 km/h (123 mph).

CHRYSLER (FRANCE)
SIMCA 1100 LE
1118 cm³

Engine—water-cooled, 4-cylinder, in-line, front mounted, bore x stroke 74 x 65, displacement 1118 cm³, ohv, compression ratio 9.6:1, max. power 43 kW (58 bhp) at 6000/min, max. torque 84.4 Nm (62 lbf.ft) at 3200/min, 1 Solex single carburettor.
Transmission—front wheels; 4-speed gearbox.
Steering—rack and pinion.
Suspension—front/rear independent wishbones with anti-roll bar, independent trailing arms.
Springs—front: longitudinal torsion bars, rear: transversal torsion bars, telescopic shock absorbers front and rear.
Brakes—front/rear discs/drums.
Dimensions and weights—length 3944mm, width 1588mm height 1458mm, wheelbase 2520mm, kerb weight 910 kg.
Tyres—145 SR 13.
Capacities—engine sump 3.3 litres (5.75 Imp. pints), cooling system 6 litres (10.50 Imp. pints), fuel tank 42 litres (9.25 Imp. gal).
   Notes—Top speed 138 km/h (86 mph).

CHRYSLER (FRANCE)
SIMCA 1308 GT/ALPINE
1442 cm^3

Engine—water-cooled, 4-cylinder, in-line, front mounted, bore x stroke 76.7 x 78, displacement 1442 cm^3, ohv, compression ratio 9.5:1, max. power 63 kW (86 bhp) at 5600/min, max. torque 125 Nm (92 lbf.ft) at 3000/min, 1 Weber single carburettor.
Transmission—front wheels; 4-speed gearbox.
Steering—rack and pinion.
Suspension—front/rear independent wishbones with anti-roll bar/independent trailing arms.
Springs—front: longitudinal torsion bars, rear: coil springs, telescopic shock absorbers front and rear.
Brakes—front/rear discs/drums, servo-assisted.
Dimensions and weights—length 4245mm, width 1680mm height 1390mm, wheelbase 2604mm, kerb weight 1075kg.
Tyres—
Capacities—engine sump 3.3 litres (5.75 Imp. pints), cooling system 6.5 litres (11.50 Imp. pints), fuel tank 60 litres (13.25 Imp. gal).
  Notes—Top speed 164 km/h (102 mph).

SKODA 120LS SUPER ESTELLE   1174 cm³

Engine—water-cooled, 4-cylinder, in-line, diesel, rear mounted, bore x stroke 72 x 72, displacement 1174 cm³, ohv, compression ratio 9.5:1, max. power 43 kW (58 bhp) at 5200/min, max. torque 90 Nm (66 lbf.ft) at 3250/min, 1 Jikov single carburettor.
Transmission—rear wheels; 4-speed gearbox.
Steering—can and lever.
Suspension—front/rear independent wishbones with anti-roll bar, independent trailing arms.
Springs—coil springs and telescopic shock absorbers front and rear.
Brakes—front/rear discs/drums, servo-assisted.
Dimensions and weights—length 4160mm, width 1595 mm, height 1400mm, wheelbase 2400mm, kerb weight 875 kg.
Tyres—155 SR 14.
Capacities—engine sump 4 litres (7 Imp. pints), cooling system 12.5 litres (22 Imp. pints), fuel tank 38 litres (8.25 Imp. gal).
  Notes—Top speed 150 km/h (93 mph)

SUBARU 1600 DL 4x4 COMBI   1595 cm^3

Engine—water-cooled, 4-cylinder, flat engine, front mounted
bore x stroke 92 x 60, displacement 1595 cm^3, ohv,
compression ratio 8.5:1, max. power 53 kW (72 bhp) at
5200/min, max. torque 113 Nm (83 lbf.ft) at 2400/min,
2 Hitachi carburettors.
Transmission—all wheels; 4-speed gearbox.
Steering—rack and pinion.
Suspension—front/rear McPherson struts with anti-roll
bar, independent trailing arms.
Springs—front: coil springs, rear: torsion bars, telescopic
shock absorbers front and rear.
Brakes—front/rear discs/drums, servo-assisted.
Dimensions and weights—length 4025mm, width 1550mm
height 1440mm, wheelbase 2450mm, kerb weight 975 kg.
Tyres—155 SR13.
Capacities—engine sump 3.6 litres (6.25 Imp. pints),
cooling system 6 litres (10.50 Imp. pints), fuel tank 45
litres (10 Imp. gal).
   Notes—Top speed 161 km/h (100 mph).

TOYOTA STARLET 993 cm^3

Engine—water-cooled, 4-cylinder, in-line, front mounted, bore x stroke 72 x 61, displacement 993 cm^3, 1 ohv, compression ratio 9:1, max. power 35 kW (48 bhp) at 5800/min, max. torque 67 Nm (49 lbf.ft) at 3800/min, 1 Aisan carburettor.

Transmission—rear wheels; 4-speed gearbox.

Steering—rack and pinion.

Suspension—front/rear McPherson struts with anti-roll bar/dead axle.

Springs—coil springs and telescopic shock absorbers front and rear.

Brakes—front/rear discs/drums, servo-assisted.

Dimensions and weights—length 3680mm, width 1525 mm, height 1380mm, wheelbase 2300mm, kerb weight 720 kg.

Tyres—145 SR 13.

Capacities—engine sump 3.5 litres (6.25 Imp. pints), cooling system 5.2 litres (9.25 Imp. pints), fuel tank 40 litres (8.75 Imp. gal).

Notes—Top speed 140 km/h (87 mph)

TOYOTA COROLLA
SPORTSWAGON 1600 GSL $1588\ cm^3$

Engine—water-cooled, 4-cylinder, in-line, front mounted,
bore x stroke 85 x 70, displacement 1588 cm^3, ohv,
compression ratio 9.4:1, max. power 60 kW (82 bhp) at
5400/min, max. torque 116 Nm (86 lbf.ft) at 4000/min,
2 carburettors.
Transmission—rear wheels; 5-speed gearbox.
Steering—recirculating ball.
Suspension—front/rear McPherson struts with anti-roll
bar/dead axle.
Springs—front: coil springs, rear: leaf springs, telescopic
shock absorbers front and rear.
Brakes—front/rear discs/drums, servo-assisted.
Dimensions and weights—length 4120mm, width 1600mm
height 1320mm, wheelbase 2370mm, kerb weight 950 kg.
Tyres—175/70 HR 13.
Capacities—engine sump 4.1 litres (7.25 Imp. pints),
cooling system 7.9 litres (14 Imp. pints), fuel tank 50
litres (11 Imp. gal).
  Notes—Top speed 155 km/h (96 mph).

TOYOTA CARINA 1600
STATIONWAGON De Luxe   1588 cm^3

Engine—water-cooled, 4-cylinder, in-line, front mounted,
bore x stroke 85 x 70, displacement 1588 cm^3, ohv,
compression ratio 9:1, max. power 55 kW (75 bhp) at
5200/min, max. torque 116 Nm (86 lbf.ft) at 3800/min,
1 Aisan single carburettor.
Transmission—rear wheels; 4-speed gearbox.
Steering—recirculating ball.
Suspension—front/rear McPherson struts with anti-roll
bar/dead axle.
Springs—coil springs and telescopic shock absorbers front
and rear.
Brakes—front/rear discs/drums, servo-assisted.
Dimensions and weights—length 4250mm, width 1630mm
height 1400mm, wheelbase 2495mm, kerb weight 980 kg.
Tyres—165 SR 13.
Capacities—engine sump 4.2 litres (7.50 Imp. pints),
cooling system 7.9 litres (14 Imp. pints), fuel tank 61
litres (13.50 Imp. gal).
  Notes—Top speed 155 km/h (96 mph).

TOYOTA CELICA
GT 2000 LIFTBACK

1968 cm^3

Engine—water-cooled, 4-cylinder, in-line, front mounted, bore x stroke 88.5 x 80, displacement 1968 cm^3, dohc, compression ratio 9.7:1, max. power 87 kW (118 bhp) at 5800/min, max. torque 152 Nm (112 lbf.ft) at 5200/min, 2 Solex double carburettors.
Transmission—rear wheels; 5-speed gearbox.
Steering—recirculating ball.
Suspension—front/rear independent wishbones with anti-roll bar/dead axle.
Springs—coil springs and telescopic shock absorbers front and rear.
Brakes—front/rear discs/drums, servo-assisted.
Dimensions and weights—length 4330mm, width 1640mm height 1310mm, wheelbase 2500mm, kerb weight 1060kg.
Tyres—185/70 HR14.
Capacities—engine sump 4 litres (7 Imp. pints), cooling system 9.1 litres (16 Imp. pints), fuel tank 61 litres (13.50 Imp. gal).
   Notes—Top speed 190 km/h (118 mph).

TOYOTA CRESSIDA De Luxe Hardtop   1968 cm^3

Engine—water-cooled, 4-cylinder, in-line, front mounted, bore x stroke 88.5 x 80, displacement 1968 cm^3, ohv, compression ratio 8.5:1, max. power 65 kW (88 bhp) at 5000/min, max. torque 145 Nm (107 lbf.ft) at 3600/min 1 Aisan single carburettor.
Transmission—rear wheels; 4-speed gearbox.
Steering—recirculating ball, servo-assisted.
Suspension—front/rear McPherson struts with anti-roll bar, dead axle with Panhard rod.
Springs—coil springs and telescopic shock absorbers front and rear.
Brakes—front/rear discs/drums, servo-assisted.
Dimensions and weights—length 4530mm, width 1680mm height 1390mm, wheelbase 2645mm, kerb weight 1130kg.
Tyres—175 SR 14.
Capacities—engine sump 5 litres (8.75 Imp. pints), cooling system 8.2 litres (14.50 Imp. pints), fuel tank 65 litres (14.25 Imp. gal).
  Notes—Top speed 160 km/h (99 mph).

TOYOTA CROWN 2600 Super Saloon   2563 cm^3

Engine—water-cooled, 6-cylinder, in-line, front mounted, bore x stroke 80 x 65, displacement 2563 cm^3, ohc, compression ratio 9.2:1, max. power 88 kW (120 bhp) at 5000/min, max. torque 194 Nm (143 lbf.ft) at 3200/min, 1 Aisan double carburettor.

Transmission—rear wheels; automatic transmission.

Steering—recirculating ball, servo-assisted.

Suspension—front/rear independent wishbones with anti-roll bar/dead axle.

Springs—coil springs and telescopic shock absorbers front and rear.

Brakes—front/rear discs/drums, servo-assisted.

Dimensions and weights—length 4765mm, width 1695mm height 1435mm, wheelbase 2690mm, kerb weight 1422kg.

Tyres—185 SR 14.

Capacities—engine sump 6.13 litres (10.75 Imp. pints), cooling system 11 litres (19.25 Imp. pints), fuel tank 72 litres (15.75 Imp. gal).

   Notes—Top speed 165 km/h (102 mph).

TOYOTA LANDCRUISER HARDTOP   4230 cm^3

Engine—water-cooled, 6-cylinder, in-line, front mounted, bore x stroke 94 x 101.6, displacement 4230 cm^3, ohv, compression ratio 7.8:1, max. power 99 kW (135 bhp) at 3600/min, max. torque 285 Nm (210 lbf.ft) at 1800/min, 1 Aisan carburettor.
Transmission—all wheels; with high and low gearing; 4-speed gearbox.
Steering—recirculating ball.
Suspension—front/rear independent wishbones, dead axle.
Springs—leaf springs and telescopic shock absorbers front and rear.
Brakes—front/rear drums/drums, servo-assisted.
Dimensions and weights—length 3990mm, width 1670mm height 1950mm, wheelbase 2280mm, kerb weight 1660kg.
Tyres—750-16 6 pr.
Capacities—engine sump 8.1 litres (14.25 Imp. pints), cooling system 18.8 litres (33 Imp. pints), fuel tank 62 litres (13.50 Imp. gal).
  Notes—Top speed 130 km/h (81 mph).

TRIUMPH DOLOMITE 1850HL   1854 cm^3

Engine—water-cooled, 4-cylinder, in-line, front mounted,
bore x stroke 87 x 78, displacement 1854 cm^3, ohc,
compression ratio 9:1, max. power 68 kW (92 bhp) at
5200/min, max. torque 142 Nm (105 lbf.ft) at 3500/min
2 SU carburettors.
Transmission—rear wheels; 4-speed gearbox.
Steering—rack and pinion.
Suspension—front/rear independent wishbones with anti-
roll bar/independent trailing arms.
Springs—coil springs and telescopic shock absorbers front
and rear.
Brakes—front/rear discs/drums, servo-assisted.
Dimensions and weights—length 4125mm, width 1570mm
height 1370mm, wheelbase 2455mm, kerb weight 970 kg.
Tyres—155 SR13.
Capacities—engine sump 4.5 litres (8 Imp. pints), cooling
system 5.4 litres (9.50 Imp. pints), fuel tank 57 litres
(12.50 Imp. gal).
  Notes—Top speed 161 km/h (100 mph)

TRIUMPH SPITFIRE 1500   1493 cm^3

Engine—water-cooled, 4-cylinder, in-line, front mounted, bore x stroke 73.7 x 87.5, displacement 1493 cm^3, ohv, compression ratio 9:1, max. power 53 kW (72 bhp) at 5500/min, max. torque 111 Nm (82 lbf.ft) at 3000/min, 2 SU carburettors.
Transmission—rear wheels; 4-speed gearbox.
Steering—rack and pinion.
Suspension—front/rear independent wishbones with anti-roll bar, independent transversal trailing arms.
Springs—front: coil spring, rear: transversal leaf springs and telescopic shock absorbers front and rear.
Brakes—front/rear discs/drums.
Dimensions and weights—length 3780mm, width 1490mm height 1160mm, wheelbase 2110mm, kerb weight 763 kg.
Tyres—155 SR 13.
Capacities—engine sump 4.5 litres (8 Imp. pints), cooling system 4.5 litres (8 Imp. pints), fuel tank 33 litres (7.25 Imp. gal).
  Notes—Top speed 161 km/h (100 mph).

TRIUMPH TR7 $\qquad$ 1998 cm^3

Engine—water-cooled, 4-cylinder, in-line, front mounted, bore x stroke 90.3 x 78, displacement 1998 cm^3, ohc, compression ratio 9.3:1, max. power 78 kW (106 bhp) at 5500/min, max. torque 163 Nm (120 lbf.ft) at 3500/min, 2 SU carburettors.
Transmission—rear wheels; 4-speed gearbox.
Steering—rack and pinion.
Suspension—front/rear McPherson struts with anti-roll bar/Dead axle.
Springs—coil springs, telescopic shock absorbers front and rear.
Brakes—front/rear discs/drums, servo-assisted.
Dimensions and weights—length 1600mm, width 1268mm height 1268mm, wheelbase 2160mm, kerb weight 1015kg.
Tyres—175/70 SR13.
Capacities—engine sump 4.5 litres (8 Imp. pints), cooling system 7.9 litres (14 Imp. pints), fuel tank 54.5 litres (12 Imp. gal).

  Notes—Top speed 172 km/h (107 mph)

TVR 3000 TAIMAR
2994 cm^3

Engine—water-cooled, 6-cylinder, front mounted, bore x stroke 73.67 x 72.42, displacement 2994 cm^3, ohv, compression ratio 8.9:1, max. power 104.5 kW (142 bhp) at 5000/min, max. torque 235 Nm (173 lbf.ft) at 3000/min, 1 Weber double carburettor.
Transmission—rear wheels; 4-speed gearbox.
Steering—rack and pinion.
Suspension—front/rear independent wishbones with anti-roll bar, independent trailing arms.
Springs—coil springs and telescopic shock absorbers front and rear.
Brakes—front/rear discs/drums, servo-assisted.
Dimensions and weights—length 4165mm, width 1625mm height 1220mm, wheelbase 2285mm, kerb weight 1000kg.
Tyres—185 HR 14.
Capacities—engine sump 5.4 litres (9.50 Imp. pints), cooling system 11.3 litres (20 Imp. pints), fuel tank 68 litres (15 Imp. gal).
   Notes—Top speed 200 km/h (124 mph).

VAUXHALL CHEVETTE GL   1256 cm^3

Engine—water-cooled, 4-cylinder, in-line, front mounted, bore x stroke 81 x 61, displacement 1256 cm^3, ohv, compression ratio 9.2:1, max. power 42.7 kW (58 bhp) at 5600/min, max. torque 89.2 Nm (66 lbf.ft) at 2600/min, 1 Zenith/Stromberg single carburettor.
Transmission—rear wheels; 4-speed gearbox.
Steering—rack and pinion.
Suspension—front/rear independent wishbones with anti-roll bar/dead axle with Panhard rod.
Springs—coil springs and telescopic shock absorbers front and rear.
Brakes—front/rear discs/drums, servo-assisted.
Dimensions and weights—length 3940mm, width 1580 mm, height 1310mm, wheelbase 2390mm, kerb weight 845 kg.
Tyres—155 SR 13.
Capacities—engine sump 2.8 litres (5 Imp. pints), cooling system 5.8 litres (10.25 Imp. pints), fuel tank 43 litres (9.50 Imp. gal).
  Notes—Top speed 146 km/h (91 mph)

VAUXHALL CAVALIER 2000 GL   1979 cm^3

Engine—water-cooled, 4-cylinder, in-line, front mounted, bore x stroke 95 x 69.8, displacement 1979 cm^3, ohc, compression ratio 9:1, max. power 74 kW (101 bhp) at 5200/min, max. torque 153 Nm (113 lbf.ft) at 3400-3800/min, 1 Zenith/Stromberg single carburettor.
Transmission—rear wheels; 4-speed gearbox.
Steering—rack and pinion.
Suspension—front/rear independent wishbones with anti-roll bar/dead axle with Panhard rod.
Springs—coil springs and telescopic shock absorbers front and rear.
Brakes—front/rear discs/drums, servo-assisted.
Dimensions and weights—length 4440mm, width 1650 mm, height 1320mm, wheelbase 2520mm, kerb weight 1010 kg.
Tyres—165 SR 13.
Capacities—engine sump 3.5 litres (6.25 Imp. pints), cooling system 7 litres (12.25 Imp. pints), fuel tank 50 litres (11 Imp. gal).

  Notes—Top speed 175 km/h (109 mph)

VAUXHALL CARLTON   1979 cm^3

Engine—water-cooled, 4-cylinder, in-line, front mounted, bore x stroke 95 x 69.8, displacement 1979 cm^3, ohv, compression ratio 9.0:1, max. power 74 kW (101 bhp at 5400/min, max. torque 153 Nm (113 lbft) at 3800/min, single GM Veri-jet carburettor.
Transmission—rear wheels, 4-speed gearbox, automatic transmission optional.
Steering—recirculating ball.
Suspension—front/rear McPherson struts, independent wishbones with anti-roll bar, independent trailing arms, live axle with anti-roll bar.
Springs—coil springs and telescopic shock absorbers front and rear.
Brakes—front/rear discs/drums, servo-assisted.
Dimensions and weights—length 4743mm, width 1726mm, height 1362mm, wheelbase 2668mm, kerb weight 1130kg.
Tyres—175 SR 14.
Capacities—engine sump 3.8 litres (6.7 Imp. pints), cooling system 6.3 litres (10.9 Imp. pints), fuel tank 65 litres (14.3 Imp. gal).
  Notes—Top speed 173 km/h (107 mph)

VOLKSWAGEN POLO N $895\ cm^3$

Engine—water-cooled, 4-cylinder, in-line, front mounted, bore x stroke 69.5 x 59, displacement 895 cm^3, ohc, compression ratio 8:1, max. power 29 kW (39 bhp) at 5900/min, max. torque 62 Nm (46 lbf.ft) at 3500/min, 1 Solex single carburettor.
Transmissiin—front wheels; 4-speed gearbox.
Steering—rack and pinion.
Suspension—front/rear McPherson struts with anti-roll bar/independent trailing arms.
Springs—coil springs and telescopic shock absorbers front and rear.
Brakes—front/rear discs/drums.
Dimensions and weights—length 3500mm, width 1559mm height 1344mm, wheelbase 2330mm, kerb weight 685 kg.
Tyres—135 SR 13.
Capacities—engine sump 3 litres (5.25 Imp. pints), cooling system 6.5 litres (11.50 Imp. pints), fuel tank 36 litres (8 Imp. gal).
  Notes—Top speed 130 km/h (81 mph).

VOLKSWAGEN DERBY LS   1272 cm^3

Engine—water-cooled, 4-cylinder, in-line, front mounted,
bore x stroke 75 x 72, displacement 1272 cm^3, 1 ohc,
compression ratio 8.2:1, max. power 44 kW (60 bhp) at
5600/min, max. torque 93 Nm (69 lbf.ft) at 3400/min,
1 Solex single carburettor.
Transmission—front wheels; 4-speed gearbox.
Steering—rack and pinion.
Suspension—front/rear McPherson struts with anti-roll
bar/independent trailing arms.
Springs—coil springs and telescopic shock absorbers
front and rear.
Brakes—front/rear, discs/drums, servo-assisted.
Dimensions and weights—length 3825mm, width 1559mm
height 1350mm, wheelbase 2335mm, kerb weight 700 kg
Tyres—145 SR 13.
Capacities—engine sump 3 litres (5.25 Imp. pints), cooling
system 6.5 litres (11.50 Imp. pints), fuel tank 36 litres
(8 Imp. gal).
  Notes—GLS version illustrated.
  Notes—Top speed 150 km/h (93 mph)

VOLKSWAGEN GOLF GTI $\qquad$ 1588 cm^3

Engine—water-cooled, 4-cylinder, in-line, front mounted, bore x stroke 79.5 x 80, displacement 1588 cm^3, ohc, compression ratio 9.5:1, max. power 81 kW (110 bhp) at 6100/min, max. torque 137.3 Nm (101 lbf.ft) at 5000/min, fuel injection Bosch K-Jetronic.
Transmission—front wheels; 4-speed gearbox.
Steering—rack and pinion.
Suspension—front/rear McPherson struts, independent wishbones with anti-roll bar/independent trailing arms.
Springs—coil springs and telescopic shock absorbers front and rear.
Brakes—front/rear discs / drums, servo-assisted.
Dimensions and weights—length 3735mm, width 1630mm height 1390mm, wheelbase 2400mm, kerb weight 810kg
Tyres—175/70 HR 13
Capacities—engine sump 3 litres (5.25 Imp. pints), cooling system 6.5 litres (11.50 Imp. pints), fuel tank 45 litres (10 Imp. gal).

   Notes—Top speed 182 km/h (113 mph)

VOLKSWAGEN PASSAT GLS Comfort   1588 cm³

Engine—water-cooled, 4-cylinder, in-line, front mounted, bore x stroke 79.5 x 80, displacement 1588 cm³, ohc, compression ratio 8.2:1, max. power 55 kW (75 bhp) at 5600/min, max. torque 119 Nm (88 lbf.ft) at 3200/min, 1 Solex single carburettor.
Transmission—front wheels; 4-speed gearbox.
Steering—rack and pinion.
Suspension—front/rear McPherson struts with anti-roll bar/dead axle with Panhard rod.
Springs—coil springs and telescopic shock absorbers front and rear.
Brakes—front/rear discs/drums, servo-assisted.
Dimensions and weights—length 4290mm, width 1615mm height 1360mm, wheelbase 2470mm, kerb weight 885 kg.
Tyres—155 SR 13.
Capacities—engine sump 3 litres (5.25 Imp. pints), cooling system 6.5 litres (11.50 Imp. pints), fuel tank 45 litres (10 Imp. gal).
  Notes—Top speed 170 km/h (106 mph).

VOLKSWAGEN SCIROCCO GT   1588 cm^3

Engine—water-cooled, 4-cylinder, in-line, front mounted, bore x stroke 79.5 x 80, displacement 1588 cm^3, ohc, compression ratio 8.2:1, max. power 63 kW (86 bhp) at 5600/min, max. torque 124 Nm (91 lbf.ft) at 3200/min, 1 Soles single carburettor.
Transmission—front wheels; 4-speed gearbox.
Steering—rack and pinion.
Suspension—front/rear McPherson struts/independent trailing arms.
Springs—coil springs and telescopic shock absorbers front and rear.
Brakes—front/rear discs/drums, servo-assisted.
Dimensions and weights—length 3875mm, width 1625mm height 1310mm, wheelbase 2400mm, kerb weight 800 kg.
Tyres—155 SR 13.
Capacities—engine sump 3 litres (5.25 Imp. pints), cooling system 4.5 litres (8 Imp. pints), fuel tank 40 litres (8.75 Imp. gal).
   Notes—Top speed 175 km/h (109 mph).

VOLVO 343 DL

1397 cm^3

Engine—water-cooled, 4-cylinder, in-line, front mounted, bore x stroke 76 x 77, displacement 1397 cm^3, ohv, compression ratio 9.5:1, max. power 51 kW (69 bhp) at 5500/min, max. torque 108 Nm (80 lbf.ft) at 3500/min, 1 Weber carburettor.
Transmission—rear wheels; 4-speed gearbox.
Steering—rack and pinion.
Suspension—front/rear McPherson struts with anti-roll bar/De Dion axle.
Springs—front coil springs, rear leaf springs and telescopic shock absorbers front and rear.
Brakes—front/rear discs/drums, servo-assisted.
Dimensions and weights—length 4205mm, width 1660mm height 1392mm, wheelbase 2395mm, kerb weight 980 kg
Tyres—155 SR 13
Capacities—engine sump 3.5 litres (6.25 Imp. pints), cooling system 6 litres (10.50 Imp. pints), fuel tank 45 litres (10 Imp. gal).

  Notes—Top speed 145 km/h (90 mph)

VOLVO 245 DL   2127 cm^3

Engine—water-cooled, 4-cylinder, in-line, front mounted, bore x stroke 92 x 80, displacement 2127 cm^3, ohc, compression ratio 9.3:1, max. power 79 kW (107 bhp) at 5500/min, max. torque 170 Nm (125 lbf.ft) at 2500/min, 1 Zenith/Stromberg carburettor.
Transmission—rear wheels; 4-speed gearbox.
Steering—rack and pinion.
Suspension—front/rear McPherson struts with anti-roll bar/dead axle with Panhard rod.
Springs—coil springs and telescopic shock absorbers front and rear.
Brakes—front/rear discs/discs servo-assisted.
Dimensions and weights—length 4880mm, width 1710mm height 1460mm, wheelbase 2640mm, kerb weight 1350kg.
Tyres—185 SR 14.
Capacities—engine sump 3.8 litres (6.75 Imp. pints), cooling system 9.5 litres (16.75 Imp. pints), fuel tank 60 litres (13.25 Imp. gal).
   Notes—Top speed 155 km/h (96 mph).

VOLVO 242 GT $\qquad$ 2315 cm^3

Engine—water-cooled, 4-cylinder, in-line, front mounted,
bore x stroke 96 x 80, displacement 2315 cm^3, ohc,
compression ratio 10:1, max. power 103 kW (140 bhp)
at 5750/min, max. torque 191 Nm (141 lbf.ft) at 4500/
min, Bosch CI-fuel injection.
Transmission—rear wheels; 4-speed gearbox.
Steering—rack and pinion.
Suspension—front/rear McPherson struts with anti-roll
bar/dead axle with Panhard rod.
Springs—coil springs and telescopic shock absorbers front
and rear.
Brakes—front/rear discs/discs/servo-assisted.
Dimensions and weights—length 4880mm, width 1710mm,
height 1430mm, wheelbase 2640mm, kerb weight 1340kg.
Tyres—185/70 HR 14.
Capacities—engine sump 3.8 litres (6.75 Imp. pints),
cooling system 9.5 litres (16.75 Imp. pints), fuel tank
60 litres (13.25 Imp. gal).
  Notes—Top speed 180 km/h (112 mph).

VOLVO 262 C   2664 cm^3

Engine—water-cooled, V-6, front mounted, bore x stroke
88 x 73, displacement 2664 cm^3, 2 x ohc, compression
ratio 9.5:1, max. power 109 kW (148 bhp) at 5700/min,
max. torque 218 Nm (161 lbf.ft) at 3000/min, Bosch CI-
fuel injection.
Transmission—rear wheels; automatic transmission BW.
Steering—rack and pinion, servo-assisted.
Suspension—front/rear McPherson struts with anti-roll
bar/dead axle with Panhard rod.
Springs—coil springs and telescopic shock absorbers front
and rear.
Brakes—front/rear discs/discs servo-assisted.
Dimensions and weights—length 4880mm, width 1710mm
height 1370mm, wheelbase 2650mm, kerb weight 1470kg.
Tyres—185/70 HR 14.
Capacities—engine sump 6.5 litres (11.50 Imp. pints),
cooling system 10.9 litres (19.25 Imp. pints), fuel tank
60 litres (13.25 Imp. gal).
  Notes—Top speed 170 km/h (105 mph).

ZASTAVA 1100 1116 cm^3

Engine—water-cooled, 4-cylinder, in-line, front mounted, bore x stroke 80 x 55.5, displacement 1116 cm^3, ohc, compression ratio 8.8:1, max. power 40.5 kW (55 bhp) at 6000/min, max. torque 80 Nm (59 lbf.ft) at 3000/min single carburettor.
Transmission—front wheels; 4-speed gearbox.
Suspension—front/rear independent wishbones with anti-roll bar, dead axle.
Springs—front coil springs , rear transversal leaf spring and telescopic shock absorbers front and rear.
Steering—rack and pinion.
Brakes—front discs.
Dimensions and weights—length 3836mm, width 1590mm height 1372mm, wheelbase 2449mm, kerb weight 842 kg
Tyres—145 SR 13
Capacities—engine sump 42.5 litres (7.50 Imp. pints), cooling system 6.5 litres (11.50 Imp. pints), fuel tank 38 litres (8.25 Imp. gal).

   Notes—Country of origin: Yugoslavia. Top speed 140km/h (87 mph).